SCHOOL PROJECTS FOR PENNIES

D1308142

Contributing Writers:
Suzanne Lieurance
Kelly Milner Halls
Jamie Gabriel

Contributing Content Development:
Jamie Gabriel

Consultant:
Susan A. Miller, Ph.D.

Illustrator:
George Ulrich

Publications International, Ltd.

ISBN: 0-7853-3583-8

Suzanne Lieurance, a former teacher, is now a full-time freelance writer. She is coauthor of *Kidding Around Kansas City*, a children's travel guide and activity book, and is the author of *Shoelaces*. She is a contributing editor for Tutor House, a children's software company, and has a regular online column, called Tricks of the Trade, for children's writers at Word Museum.

Kelly Milner Halls is a freelance writer whose work frequently appears in *Highlights for Children, Family Fun Magazine, Boys Life, Fox Kids,* and the *Chicago Tribune.* Her books include *Dino-Trekking* and *I Bought a Baby Chicken,* and she is the coauthor of *365 After School Activities* and *365 Outdoor Activities.* She is former coordinator of the Longmont (Colorado) YMCA after-school day-care program.

Jamie Gabriel is a freelance writer who has written and edited curriculum support material for numerous educational publishers. She served as content developer for the book *Rainy Day Crafts and Activities.*

Susan A. Miller, Ph.D., is a professor of early childhood education at Kutztown University. She has contributed to over 150 journals, magazines, and books, including *Childhood Education, Parent & Child* magazine, and *365 After School Activities.* She is the author of *Learning Through Play: Sand, Water, Wood and Clay.* She frequently gives presentations at the National Association for the Education of Young Children and the Association of Childhood Education International Study conferences.

Illustrator: George Ulrich

CONTENTS

INTRODUCTION

DEAR PARENTS AND TEACHERS—

You know your child's abilities—craft knives are very sharp and stoves can be very hot. You should judge whether the child is able to handle a hot pan safely. And even if the child is able to handle it, you should be present to prevent accidents or injuries! Occasionally instructions direct the child to ask for adult help. Be sure everyone understands the "Important Things to Know" section in this introduction.

We have given you some basic information about different topics, but this is a great opportunity for you and your child to learn more about the subjects in this book. If you have a computer, there are many Web sites you can explore together. Of course, the library is always a good place to find more information.

The projects in this book were specifically designed to be inexpensive. No project costs more than $2 to make, and most cost even less than that. Many projects are done with everyday supplies you have around the house.

This should be an enjoyable, creative experience for children. Although we provide specific instructions, it's wonderful to see children create their own versions, using their own ideas. Encourage their creativity and interests!

HEY KIDS—

With *School Projects for Pennies,* you have lots of fun ahead of you! This book is filled with exciting games to play, great gifts to make for family and friends, and terrific projects to decorate your room.

This book was made with you in mind. Many of the projects are fun things you can make by yourself. With some projects, however, you will need to ask an adult for help. Not only can an adult help you with the projects, but they can also admire your wonderful results!

It's a good idea to make a project following the instructions exactly. Then feel free to make another, using your imagination, changing colors, adding a bit of yourself to make it even more yours. Think of all the variations you can make and all the gifts you can give!

If you're curious about the topics mentioned in this book, do some exploring to find out more. Ask an adult to help you research—try the Internet (with adult permission, of course) and the library. Having some information makes you want more information—expand your world with knowledge!

The most important thing you need to remember is to have fun! Think how proud you'll be to say, "I made this myself!"

KEY—

Each project is rated as to its challenge level. Look for the difficulty level written on the small chalkboards at the top of each project. We have also added plus marks for those projects that are a bit harder but don't quite qualify for the next level.

EASY MEDIUM DIFFICULT

IMPORTANT THINGS TO KNOW—

Although we know you'll want to get started right away, please read these few basic steps before beginning any project.

1. For any project or activity you decide to do, gather all your materials, remembering to ask permission first! If you need to purchase materials, take along your book or make a shopping list so you know exactly what you need.

2. Prepare your work area ahead of time. Clean up will be easier if you prepare first!

3. Be sure that an adult is nearby to offer help if you need it. An adult is needed if you will be using a glue gun, a craft knife, the oven, or anything else that may be dangerous!

4. Be careful not to put any materials near your mouth. Watch out for small items, such as beads, around little kids and pets. And keep careful watch of balloons and any broken balloon pieces. These are choking hazards—throw away any pieces immediately! Small children should not play with balloons unless an adult is present.

5. Use the glue gun set on the low-temperature setting. Do not touch the nozzle or the freshly applied glue; it may still be hot. Use the glue gun with adult permission only!

6. Wear an apron when painting with acrylic paints; after the paint dries, it is permanent. If you do get paint on your clothes, wash them with soap and warm water immediately.

7. Cover your work surface with newspaper or a old, plastic tablecloth. Ask an adult if you're not sure whether to cover the kitchen table—but remember, it's better to be safe than sorry!

8. Clean up afterward, and put away all materials and tools. Leaving a mess one time may mean that Mom says "No" the next time you ask to make something!

9. Have fun, and be creative!

SCIENCE SAFARI

Scientists probe the questions of how things work and why things act the way they do. But science is not just for scientists. Everyone is interested in the world around them and what makes things tick.

You can learn a great deal about your world by observing and performing experiments right in your own backyard or kitchen. Here are some activities to get you started investigating at home!

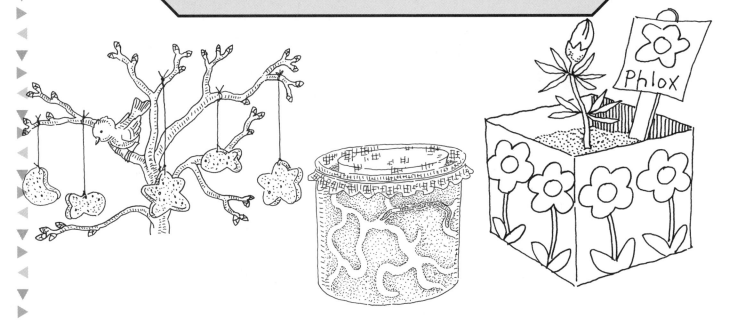

SPACE HELMET

Practice "walking on the moon" in your own backyard with this cool space helmet, complete with its own make-believe oxygen tanks.

EASY

Adult Help Needed

WHAT YOU'LL NEED

Paper grocery bag
Crayons or markers
Scissors
2 oatmeal boxes
2 paper towel tubes
Tape or stapler and staples

Put a paper grocery bag over your head. Using a marker, have a friend trace a circle on the bag where your face is. Take the bag off your head, and cut out the circle. You may also want to cut the bag around your shoulders so it is more comfortable to wear.

In the middle of each oatmeal box lid, trace the end of a paper towel tube. Cut out the hole (have an adult help you with this, if necessary).

Staple or tape the oatmeal boxes side by side to the back of your helmet, lid side up. Stick an end of each paper towel tube through the top of each oatmeal box. Tape the top of each tube to the helmet so the tubes look like oxygen tank hoses.

Decorate your helmet so it looks like one on a real space suit—or you can make your helmet look like one on an alien space suit. Use your imagination! Put on your new space helmet, and do your best moon walk.

Space Dust

Did you know that gravity on the moon is only one-sixth as powerful as on Earth? The first moonwalkers, astronauts Neil Armstrong and Buzz Aldrin, reported that when they kicked dust with their boots, every grain landed almost exactly the same distance away!

BUTTERFLY NET

Make your own net to capture butterflies and other small creatures for examination and study. This net won't hurt them; they can be safely released.

MEDIUM

WHAT YOU'LL 👀 NEED 👀

Plastic mesh bag
   (such as the bag
   onions come in)
Scissors
Chenille stems
Tape
Long cardboard tube
Scissors

Optional:
Drawing paper
Markers or crayons
Butterfly reference
   books from the
   library

Cut the clamp off the end of a mesh onion bag (leave an end clamped). Next, make a rim for the net by fastening 2 chenille together by twisting the ends. Thread the stems in and out along the top edge of the mesh bag. When you're finished, secure the ends of the rim with a piece of tape.

For a handle, use a very stiff cardboard tube (like the kind found in a roll of wrapping paper). On 1 end of the tube, cut a slit on each side. Insert the rim of the net into the slits, and tape it in place.

Now it's time to go out and explore the natural world. When you find and capture a butterfly, examine it quickly and then draw it. After you let the butterfly fly to freedom, you can look up the butterfly in a book to determine what type it is and more about it. Collect several pages of drawings, and make your own butterfly book.

You'll be a butterfly expert in no time!

LEONARDO DA SALTY

Use science and salt to make amazing pictures!

WHAT YOU'LL NEED
Newspaper
Warm water
Salt
Several containers
Food coloring
Paper
Paintbrushes or
    cotton swabs

Salt and food color will both dissolve in water, which is a physical change. If the water evaporates, the salt and the food color are left behind, which is also a physical change. Use these physical changes (which make a substance look different but don't change the chemistry of the objects) to make great art!

Cover your work surface with newspaper. Mix warm water and salt together in several containers; add as much salt to each solution as it will hold—until no more salt will dissolve. Add a few drops of different food color to each container, and mix well.

Paint a picture on paper using the colored salt solutions. Put it on thick so that when it dries a lot of salt will be left behind. Let the painted paper sit for several hours until the water evaporates, and then observe. Notice how the color and salt remain on the paper. The interesting patterns of color around the salt crystals create a beautiful picture.

BLOWING IN THE WIND

How does a weather vane work? Find out by making your own.

**WHAT YOU'LL
NEED**
Heavy cardboard
2 pencils
Ruler
Scissors
Aluminum foil
String
Nut, bolt, or other
    weight

Draw a wind vane, in the shape of an arrow, on a sheet of heavy cardboard. Your vane should be about 14 inches long and 5 inches wide, and the tail should be wider than the point. Cut the wind vane from the cardboard with scissors. Cover the arrow with aluminum foil so it can withstand the weather outside.

Balance the cardboard wind vane on the point of a pencil, and mark the spot on the wind vane where it balances. Punch 2 holes side by side in the wind vane at this balance spot; each hole should be ½ inch from the edge of the vane. Tie an 18-inch piece of string through the top hole and a 12-inch piece of string through the bottom hole. Tie a nut or bolt to the bottom piece of string for a weight. Tie the top piece of string to a tree branch where the vane can swing easily without hitting anything.

When the wind blows, your wind vane will point directly into the wind. The larger surface of the tail provides more resistance to the wind and causes the point to face into the wind.

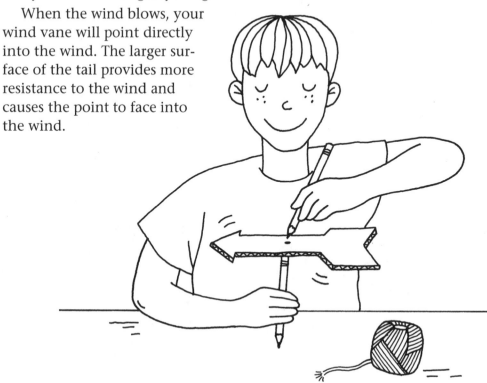

ELECTRO-DETECTO

Make a device that detects electrical charges.

WHAT YOU'LL NEED

Bottle
Cork
Nail
Electrical wire
Thin aluminum foil
Scissors
Ruler

Find a bottle and a cork that will seal it. With a nail, make a small hole through the center of the cork from top to bottom. Push a 6-inch piece of heavy electrical wire through the hole. Leave about 1 inch of wire above the top of the cork.

Bend the wire coming out from the bottom of the cork into a flat hook, shaped like the bottom of a coat hanger. Use the scissors to cut a piece of aluminum foil into a strip 1 inch long and ¼ inch wide. Fold the strip in half, and hang it on the flat hook. Put the hook and foil into the bottle, and seal the opening with the cork. Make sure the foil and the hook do not touch the sides or bottom of the jar. Roll up another piece of aluminum foil into a tight ball, about 1 inch in diameter, around the wire sticking out of the top of the cork. Make sure that the ball is smooth and tightly packed.

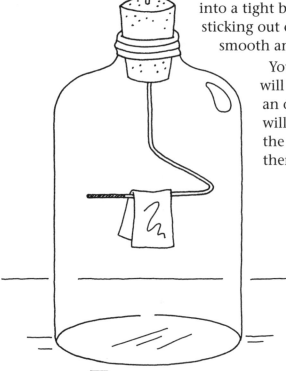

You have just built a functional electroscope that will tell you if an object carries a charge. If you hold an object with a charge near the foil ball, the object will draw the opposite charge through the wire from the foil strip. The 2 sides of the aluminum strip will then have the same charge and repel each other.

ROCKING CANDY!

*Find out that when liquids evaporate into gases,
they can leave material behind.*

WHAT YOU'LL NEED

Pan
Water
Potholder
Hot pad
Sugar
Measuring spoon
String
Pencil
Glass
Scissors
Button

Have an adult help you bring a small pan of water to a boil on the stove. Turn off the heat, and move the pan to the table (have an adult do this for you). Place the pan on a hot pad. Add 1 tablespoon of sugar, and stir until it dissolves. Continue adding sugar, 1 tablespoon at a time, letting each tablespoonful dissolve completely before adding the next. When no more sugar will dissolve in the water, allow the saturated solution to cool (be sure it is in a safe place so it can't be bumped or spilled).

Tie a string to the middle of a pencil, and set the pencil across the rim of a glass. Cut the string so that it just touches the bottom of the glass. Tie a button onto the bottom of the string. Pour the cooled sugar water into the glass. Rest the pencil across the rim of the glass so that the string and button are in the solution. Allow it to sit in a warm place without being disturbed for several days so that the water evaporates. As the water evaporates, it will leave sugar crystals on the string. You can eat these crystals like rock candy.

WILDLIFE CALENDAR

No need to buy an expensive wildlife calendar when you can have fun creating your own!

WHAT YOU'LL NEED

Newspaper (optional)
Paints or colored markers
Paintbrushes
Drawing paper
Colorful magazine pictures of nature scenes (optional)
Poster board
Ruler
Glue
Hole punch
Yarn or ribbon

Exploring nature is fun and educational! Make a record of your explorations by creating a calendar.

(If you are using paint, cover your work surface with newspaper.) With paints or colored markers, make 12 colorful drawings of different wildlife scenes from your neighborhood (for example, squirrels finding acorns, birds eating from feeders, etc.) on 12 separate sheets of paper (make 1 scene per page). If you don't like to draw or paint, you could cut out colorful magazine pictures of 12 different wildlife scenes.

Measure and cut out 12 sheets of poster board that are twice the length of your pictures (all 12 should be the same size). When you are finished, glue each drawing or picture to the top of a separate sheet of poster board. Then draw a 1-month calendar on the bottom of each piece of poster board. Punch 2 holes in the center top of each piece of poster board, and tie all the pages together with a piece of yarn or ribbon.

Now you have a complete 12-month calendar to commemorate your neighborhood wildlife!

WORKOUT STATIONS

Have fun exercising at your own workout stations—add posters
that have directions for what to do at each one.

WHAT YOU'LL
🪙🪙 NEED 🪙🪙

Sticks or pieces
   of rope
Bath mat or nonslip
   rug
Poster board
Markers
Jump rope
Canned goods (or
   paper towel
   tubes, rocks, and
   tape)
Blank cards
Transparent tape

Make 4 workout stations, each with a poster explaining what to do there. Mark off each station with sticks or pieces of rope. At the first station, place a bath mat or nonslip rug for sit-ups. The poster here should explain what a sit-up is. It should also say, "Do 10 sit-ups before moving to the next workout station."

At the second station, make a poster that explains what a push-up is, and the poster should say, "Do 10 push-ups before moving to the next workout station." The third workout station should include a jump rope. The poster at this station should say, "Jump rope 10 times before moving to the next workout station."

At the fourth station, place some canned goods to use as lightweight dumb-bells (or make your own by filling paper towel tubes with rocks and taping the ends). Make a poster that says, "Do 10 curls for each arm with the dumbbells to complete your workout."

Before you begin working out, make sure you stretch out all your muscles—do some side bends, toe touches (no bouncing), and arm stretches. When you are done stretching, start your workout routine.

After you have mastered your circuit of exercises, add 2 more reps (repetitions of the exercise) to each workstation. Tape a blank card over the number on each poster, and write in the new number. After mastering each new number, add another 2 reps. You will be the most fit kid on your block—keep those muscles active and healthy!

A Hearty Workout

Exercise helps your muscles grow stronger, but did you know that it also helps your heart? That's because your heart is actually a muscle. In fact, the heart is the strongest muscle in your body. In an average lifetime, the heart beats more than two and a half billion times, without ever pausing to rest. Since it can't lift weights to get stronger, your heart relies on you to exercise.

WORM CONDO

Worms are fascinating creatures. Watch them tunnel through the dirt, then return them to their natural environment after a few days!

WHAT YOU'LL NEED

2 clear plastic containers (one slightly smaller than the other)
Soil
Worms
Screen or piece of stocking
Rubber band

First, you'll need a clear plastic container. Place another container, an inch or so smaller in diameter, inside the larger container. You are creating a narrow enough space between the containers so you'll be able to see the worms tunnel.

Fill the space between the 2 containers with a good supply of fresh soil (not potting soil), and keep it moist (but not soaked). Put in some worms, then cover the container with a piece of screen or stocking for good air flow. Secure this cover with a rubber band.

Now watch the worms as they tunnel through the soil! (Be sure to keep this out of the hot sun, and free the worms after a few days of observation.)

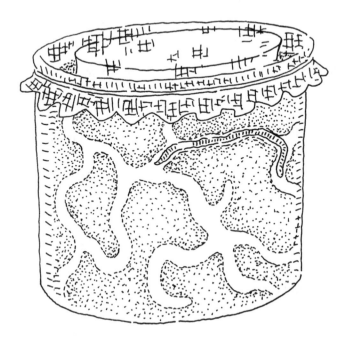

SOUND WAVE MODEL

Use this model to find out how sounds move through the air.

WHAT YOU'LL NEED

Thread
Scissors
Ruler
6 metal ball bearings
Tape
Clothes hanger

Cut 6 pieces of thread, each 10 inches long, and attach an end of each thread to a ball bearing using tape. Tie the other end of each thread to the horizontal piece of a clothes hanger, leaving about 1 inch between each thread that you tie.

Hang the hook of the clothes hanger from a shower-curtain rod. Pull back 1 of the end bearings. Let the bearing go so that it strikes the next one. Watch what happens. It hits the second, which swings and hits the third, and so on.

Sound travels through the air in the same way. A vibration causes 1 molecule of air to move and bump into another molecule, which then moves at the same rate and bumps into a third molecule, and so on.

ANIMAL LITTER BAGS

These handy litter bags are decorated to look like animals, so you "feed the animals" each time you throw away trash.

EASY

Adult Help Needed

WHAT YOU'LL 👀 NEED 👀

Stapler
Paper grocery bags
Scissors
Crayons or markers
Construction paper
Tape or glue
Work gloves

Staple the top of a large grocery bag closed. Then, on the plain side of the paper bag, cut out a large opening that will be the mouth of your animal. Be sure the mouth is high enough on the bag so it will still hold trash.

Color eyes, ears, nose, and feet on the bag to look like any animal you choose. If you'd like, use construction paper and cut out shapes for the body parts. Tape or glue them onto the bag in the proper places. You can also cut strips of paper for fur or a mane, and glue them to the bag. Use your imagination—your creation doesn't have to be an animal you've ever seen before!

When your animal is completed, put on your work gloves and walk around your yard or neighborhood. Pick up litter, and put it in the bag through the animal's mouth. Don't pick up any broken glass, needles, or other dangerous materials. Have an adult come along on your garbage hunt to help out with those things!

CHOOSE A COMPASS

Make a compass, and you'll always know in what direction you've headed. You can make either a floating compass or a Chinese hanging compass—or both!

WHAT YOU'LL NEED

2 needles
Magnet
Cork
Scissors
2 clear plastic cups
Water
Thread
Pencil

Rub the pointed end of the needle along a side of the magnet, always rubbing in the same direction. Do this about 30 times to magnetize the needle. You can test it by picking up a pin with it. If you will be making both compasses, repeat the process with the other needle.

Floating Compass: Cut a small piece of cork, and push the magnetized needle through it. Fill a plastic cup with water. Carefully place the cork with the magnetized needle into the cup so it floats in the center. The magnetized end will always face north.

Chinese Hanging Compass: Tie an end of a short piece of thread to the center of the magnetized needle, and tie the other end of the thread to a pencil. Place the pencil over the rim of the plastic cup. Again, the magnetized end of the needle will point north.

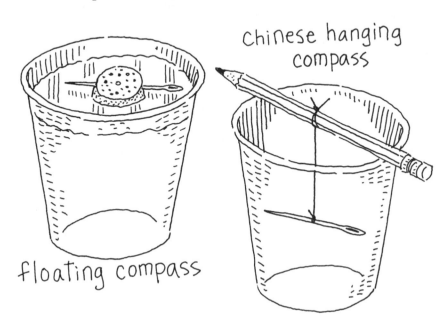

chinese hanging compass

floating compass

LIFE ON A BRICK

It's amazing; you can grow grass on a brick!

WHAT YOU'LL NEED

Nonglazed porous brick
Bowl
Water
Pie tin
Grass seed

Many plants can adapt to very difficult growing conditions. Grass seeds, for example, can sprout in less than ideal locations. Soak a nonglazed brick overnight in a bowl of water. The next day, put the brick in a pie tin. Set the pie tin in a sunny spot. Pour water over the brick so that it runs down into the tin until the brick is sitting in about ½ inch of water. Sprinkle grass seed on the top of the brick. The grass seed will sprout into plants.

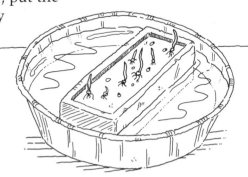

PRECIOUS BELONGINGS POUCH

Make this pouch to carry all the precious belongings you'll collect as you go exploring on field trips or nature walks.

WHAT YOU'LL NEED

Different colored sheets of felt
Scissors
Ruler
Staples or glue

Cut a 5×12-inch rectangle out of a piece of felt. Fold up the long end of the strip about ⅔ of the way. Staple or glue the edges together to form a pocket. If you'd like, you can make 2 parallel slits in the back of the pouch so you can thread your belt through the slits. Decorate the pocket by cutting out shapes from the felt (maybe nature shapes, such as leaves, animals, flowers, etc.) and gluing them to the pocket. Now it's time for that nature walk!

SUNSHINE OVEN

Use the sun and aluminum foil to create a solar-powered oven,
and bake a delicious treat to share with a friend!

WHAT YOU'LL NEED

Aluminum foil
8 × 11-inch white
   paper
Scissors
Glue
Apple slices
Small paper cup
Plastic wrap
Rubber band
Cinnamon (optional)

This is a project for a sunny, summer day. Take the aluminum foil, and, using the white paper as a guide, cut the foil into an 8×11-inch sheet. Glue the foil to the paper, and roll it into a cone with the white paper on the outside. Let the glue dry.

Place the apple slices in the cup. Cover the top of the cup with plastic wrap, and place the rubber band around the plastic wrap to hold it in place.

Dig a small hole (ask permission first!), and place the pointed end of the cone into the hole. Make sure the cone is lined up directly with the sun. At noon, when the sun is at its hottest, set the cup with the apple slices inside the cone. Leave the cone outside for 2 hours, checking it every 30 minutes. When the apple has baked, sprinkle the slices with a little cinnamon and share this treat with a friend.

M-m-m, sunshiny good!

MILK CARTON WATERWHEEL

Newton's third law states, "Every action has an equal and opposite reaction." Have fun proving that law by making a waterwheel—but do this project outside because it is quite wet!

MEDIUM

Adult Help Needed

WHAT YOU'LL NEED

Paper milk carton
Pencil
Scissors
String
Water

This is a fun way to play with water on a hot, sunny day. Put on your thinking caps and your bathing suits! Use a pencil to poke a hole in the bottom left-hand corner of each of the 4 sides of a paper, ½-gallon milk carton. With scissors, poke a hole in the top flap of the milk carton (you may need adult help with this). Tie a string through this hole, and tie the carton to a branch or something from which it can suspend. While covering the holes in the milk carton with your fingers, have a helper pour water into the carton.

When the carton is filled, take your fingers off the holes and see what happens to the milk carton as the water flows out. You've created a waterwheel!

PERFECT PLANTER

You'll want to make several of these perfect planters from empty milk or juice cartons. Give them as gifts, or start your own nursery.

WHAT YOU'LL NEED

Empty milk or juice cartons (washed and clean)
Scissors
Construction paper
Glue or tape
Old magazines
Crayons or colored pencils
Craft stick
Potting soil
Flower seeds or seedling (young plant)

Open the top of an empty milk or juice carton. Cut the top off to make a 4- to 6-inch planter. Use construction paper to cover all 4 sides of the planter, then tape or glue the paper in place. Decorate the construction paper with magazine pictures and drawings. You could draw the flowers you will grow in your planter, or you could draw anything you want. That's where your imagination comes in handy!

Cut a small square of construction paper to make a marker. Write the name and draw a picture of the flower you will grow in the planter. Attach the marker to a craft stick with glue or tape.

Fill the planter ¾ full with potting soil. Plant the seeds in the soil, or transplant a seedling to the decorated container. Add your plant marker.

Now watch your garden grow!

SHELL PRINT

Using clay, see how a fossil print might have been made.

WHAT YOU'LL NEED

Newspaper or plastic mat

Air-drying modeling clay

Plastic or butter knife

Pencil

Small seashell (or other object to make an impression with)

Leather strip or thick yarn

Real fossils are formed in several different ways. They can be the actual hard remains of ancient organisms, parts of organisms that have been replaced by minerals, or impressions of the organisms that have been preserved in sediments. Using a shell and clay, you can imitate this process.

Cover your work surface with newspaper or a plastic mat. Start with a 3/8-inch-thick slab of air-drying modeling clay. Cut out a 2-inch-diameter circle of clay. Use a pencil to poke a hole through the top of the clay circle. Press an interesting small seashell firmly into the circle of clay. Carefully remove the shell. It should leave a clear impression. The impression will resemble a fossil imprint. Allow the clay to air dry.

Thread a leather strip or thick yarn through the hole, and tie the ends in a knot. You can wear your shell imprint around your neck.

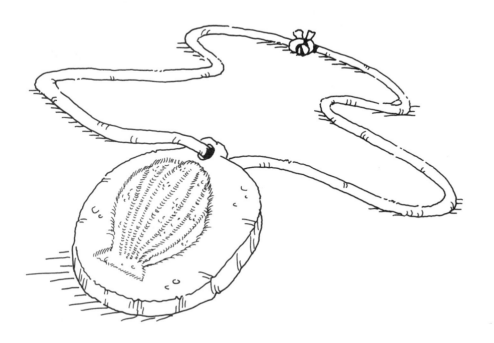

WIND WHIRL

This simple Wind Whirl, when placed over a hot lamp,
shows how heat affects the air.

**WHAT YOU'LL
NEED**

Pencil
Stiff paper
Scissors
String
Hot lamp

Draw a large spiral, like the one shown here, on a sheet of stiff paper. Following the line on the spiral, cut along it with scissors. Punch a hole through the center of the spiral. Thread a piece of string through the hole in the center of the spiral, and tie the string to the spiral's end.

You will need an adult's help with this part of the project—**do not attempt this without supervision!** Holding the string with one hand, hang the spiral over a hot lamp. Keep the end of the paper at least 2 to 3 inches away from the lamp.

What happens to the spiral, and why? The heat from the lamp warms the air, and the heated air moves upward. This rising air causes the spiral to move.

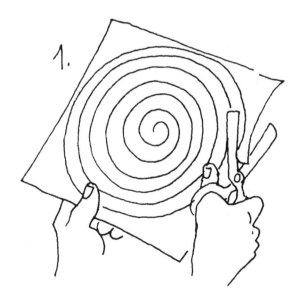

BREAKFAST FOR THE BIRDS

This breakfast is strictly for the birds—don't you taste it!

MEDIUM

Adult Help Needed

WHAT YOU'LL NEED

- 2 cups biscuit baking mix
- Water
- 2 tablespoons margarine
- 2 tablespoons sesame seeds
- 2 tablespoons sunflower seeds
- Measuring cup and spoons
- Mixing bowl
- Mixing spoon
- Rolling pin
- Cookie cutters
- Spatula
- Baking sheet
- Straw
- Small saucepan
- Pastry brush
- Fork
- Cooling rack
- Ribbon

Ask an adult to preheat the oven to 425 degrees. Add enough water (just a few tablespoons) to the baking mix to form a soft dough. Roll out the dough to ¾-inch thickness, and cut it into shapes with the cookie cutters.

Using a spatula, put the shapes on a baking sheet. Use the straw to punch a hole in the top of each cookie.

Ask an adult to melt the margarine. Brush the melted margarine over the dough. Sprinkle the seeds onto the dough, and press them in firmly with a fork.

Bake for 15 to 20 minutes or until light brown. Remove cookies with a spatula, and place them on a cooling rack.

When the cookies are cool, thread brightly colored ribbon through the holes. Hang the bird snacks in a tree. Now wait for the birds to enjoy their breakfast! (Note: If birds don't eat the biscuits right away, check after a few days to be sure the biscuits aren't moldy. If they are, remove them from the tree and make fresh ones.)

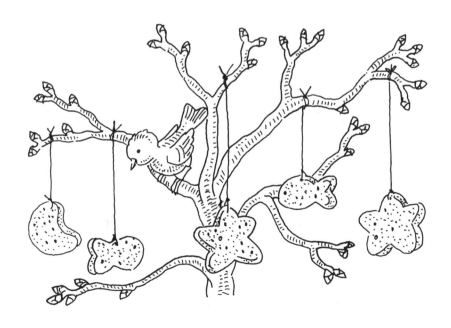

INCREDIBLE ICEBOATS

Make an iceboat, and see how long
your boat can last!

EASY

Adult Help Needed

WHAT YOU'LL NEED

Pint juice carton
Water
Measuring cups
Food coloring
Duct tape
Craft knife (adult
    use only)
12-inch wooden
    dowel
Colored cellophane
Scissors
Ruler
Tape
Large tub

Fill the carton with 1½ cups of water, and add several drops of food coloring. Seal the top of the carton with duct tape, and shake it gently. Lay the sealed carton on its side, and have an adult use a craft knife to cut a small X through the center of the side facing up. Push the dowel through the opening, and set the carton in the freezer overnight.

Cut out a cellophane sail that is 8 inches high, 7 inches across the base, and 11 inches along the diagonal. When the water is completely frozen, cut away the carton from the ice. Fold the 8-inch side of the sail around the dowel, and tape it in place.

Fill a large tub with water, and let the boat begin to float!

For more fun, have a friend make a boat at his or her house, and you make one at yours. When the boats are finished, invite your friend over to race!

THE GREAT BUG SEARCH

Go on a Great Bug Search in your own backyard, and find out where bugs and worms like to make their homes. See how much information you can gather!

WHAT YOU'LL NEED
White fabric
Stick
Notepad
Pencil
Magnifying glass

Discover secret places where insects make their homes.

Spread a piece of white fabric on the ground beneath a low-hanging branch. With a stick, give the branch a short, sharp rap. In your notepad, write down the number and kinds of insects that come tumbling down onto the fabric. Use the magnifying glass to examine the bugs closely. If you don't know the bug, draw a picture of it in your notepad and go to the library for a bit of bug sleuthing! After you've written down all the bugs, let them go without harming them.

Now roll over a rotting log, and see what you find (probably slow-moving pill bugs, sow bugs, slugs, snails, and earthworms, among others). Do you see any tiny seedlings, mosses and lichens, or mushrooms? Again, use your magnifying glass to examine the objects clearly. Write down whatever you see, then roll the log back in place. (You wouldn't want someone coming along and moving your house, would you?)

How much information did you learn about bugs?

BLUBBER BAGS

Find out how seals and whales stay warm, even in very cold water!

WHAT YOU'LL NEED

Bucket
Ice
Water
2 large plastic bags
Vegetable shortening

Do this experiment with a friend for extra fun. Fill a bucket with ice and water; make sure the water is very cold before doing the experiment.

Be sure there are no holes in the plastic bags. Fill 1 bag about half full with vegetable shortening. Have your friend slip the second bag over his or her hand, like a glove, and slide it into the shortening-filled bag. Your friend should mush the shortening around until it surrounds the hand. Now plunge your bare hand into the bucket of ice water, and hold it there for 20 to 30 seconds. After you take your hand out of the water, your friend should plunge his or her blubber glove into the ice water.

How long could your friend keep his or her gloved hand in the water? Why do you think the gloved hand stayed as warm and comfortable as a seal in the winter?

Now take your turn with the blubber bag, and see for yourself what a difference the "blubber" makes.

FINGERPRINT FUN

Have fun uncovering fingerprints with this
easy-to-make fingerprint kit!

WHAT YOU'LL NEED

Cold cream
White envelope
No. 2 pencils
Index cards
Ruler
Paper
Clear tape
Emery board
Small dish
Soft bristle paint-
    brush
Magnifying glass
    (optional)

Collect all your family members to play this fingerprint game. Have everyone gather in another room where you can't see them. Before they go, give them a jar of cold cream and 1 white envelope. Tell them that only one person should rub cold cream into his or her hands and then hold the envelope. They shouldn't tell you who does it, but you'll be able to tell by matching the fingerprints.

To Solve the Mystery: Before starting the game, you need to create a fingerprint file for each member of the family. First, write each person's name on a separate file card, and draw two 1-inch squares for the fingerprints. Rub the point of a No. 2 pencil on a separate piece of paper until you have a solid 1-inch square. Roll each person's left thumb on the square to coat it with graphite, then press it down on the sticky side of a piece of tape. Gently lift off the tape, and press it onto one of the squares on the file card. Repeat this procedure for the right-hand thumb. Be sure everyone washes their hands after being fingerprinted.

To Dust for Prints: In a small dish, make some graphite powder by rubbing a pencil point against an emery board. Dip your paintbrush into the powder, and gently brush the entire surface of the envelope to expose the hidden prints. They will appear like magic.

To Match the Prints: Examine the prints on the envelope for arches, loops, and whorls. Are there any broken lines in the ridges? Compare the dusted prints (which are backward) with the fingerprint file cards. Use a magnifying glass if you need to. This should tell you who touched the envelope.

Fingerprint Fact

In the 1800s, police needed to catch a burglar at the scene of the crime to convict him. William Herschel was the first to realize that no two people had the same fingerprints and that they could be used to identify someone. In the early 1900s, police caught a burglar for the first time using a fingerprint, which was left in wet paint.

NO-STING BUBBLES

These bubbles won't sting your eyes if you get some of the mixture near your face (which always seems to happen).

EASY

WHAT YOU'LL 👓👓 NEED 👓👓

¹/₄ cup baby shampoo (no-sting type)
³/₄ cup water
3 tablespoons light corn syrup
Measuring cups and spoons
Mixing bowl
Mixing spoon
Thin wire
Pie plate

This is a great project to do outside on a summer day!

Mix the baby shampoo, water, and light corn syrup in a bowl. Stir the ingredients gently so you don't create lots of bubbles; let the bubbles settle. Bend an end of a piece of thin wire into a circle; this is your bubble blower. Pour some of the bubble mixture into a pie plate, dip the circle into the bubble mixture, then blow to create some bubbles!

For more bubble experimentation, make other shapes out of thin wire. Make a triangle, square, hexagon, or other shape out of the thin wire. See if the bubble shapes are any different depending on the shape of the blower. You can also blow bubbles with a plastic berry basket.

Can you find any other things that would make good bubble blowers? Explore and experiment!

BATH JELLY

Here's a fascinating concoction to create in your own scientific laboratory (also known as your kitchen)! Use the bath jelly yourself, or give it as a gift to someone special.

Adult Help Needed

WHAT YOU'LL NEED

½ cup water
Measuring cup
Saucepan
Pot holder
Hot pad
1 envelope unfla-
    vored gelatin
Mixing spoon
½ cup bubble bath
    or liquid soap
Food coloring
Jar with lid
Small toy or seashells

Have an adult heat the water until it boils and then move it to the table with the pot holder, using a hot pad to protect the table. Dissolve the gelatin in the boiling water.

When the gelatin is completely dissolved, add the bubble bath or soap and a few drops of food coloring slowly. Do not beat the mixture because it may become foamy. Stir gently to blend. Pour the mixture in a jar with a lid. Drop in a small toy or some pretty seashells. Put the jar in the refrigerator to set.

To use, place a small amount of jelly under tap water for a bubble bath, or use it as a shower gel.

JIGGLY GELATIN LENSES

Make these "Jiggly Gelatin Lenses" and find out
how eyeglass lenses work.

MEDIUM

Adult Help Needed

WHAT YOU'LL NEED

Water
Small pan
Pot holder
Measuring cup
Small mixing bowl
Package of lemon,
   pineapple, or
   other light-
   colored gelatin
Mixing spoon
Variety of rounded
   containers
   (ladles, ice-
   cream scoops,
   wine glasses,
   round-bottomed
   bowls, round-
   bowl measuring
   spoons)
Tray
Clear plastic wrap
Knife (optional)
Newspaper

Have an adult help you with boiling the water on the stove. Pour the gelatin into a mixing bowl, and add 1 cup of boiling water. Stir until all the gelatin dissolves. Choose a variety of containers to pour the gelatin into; use containers with round, smooth bottoms to give the lenses smooth, curved surfaces. Set the containers on a tray, and fill them with the gelatin mixture. Put the tray into the refrigerator, and chill the gelatin for at least 4 hours or until fully set.

When the gelatin is set, wet a piece of clear plastic wrap to prevent sticking. Wet your fingers, too. Run hot tap water over the outside of the containers, and, if necessary, coax the gelatin out with the tip of a warm, wet knife. Place the lenses on the plastic wrap, flat side down.

Place the plastic wrap over a sheet of newspaper. Slide the plastic wrap slowly over the paper while looking through a lens. Try all the lenses on the same word, then look at some pictures. Which lenses make the words look bigger? Which make them look wiggly? Why do different lenses make the same thing look different?

If you'd like to do some more exploring about lenses, check out some books from your school or local library.

How Does This Experiment Work?

If you bend light before it gets into your eyes, you can change the picture of the world that forms inside your eyes. The gelatin lenses bend light to make the picture in your eye bigger, so the words and pictures in the newspaper look bigger than they really are.

SO MUCH PRESSURE!

Make a water barometer that will show you changes in air pressure.

WHAT YOU'LL NEED

2 rulers
Modeling clay
Bowl
Water
Clear plastic bottle
String
Scissors
Paper
Permanent marker
Tape

Stick a ruler into a lump of modeling clay, and put the clay and ruler in the bottom of a bowl. (The ruler should be upright.) Pour about 3 inches of water into the bowl.

Get a narrow, clear plastic bottle. Fill it about ¾ full of water. Cover the top of the bottle with your hand, turn it upside down, and put it into the bowl next to the ruler. Once the bottle top is underwater, you can take your hand away. With the bottle upside down, tie the ruler to the bottle with string.

Cut a strip of paper 4 inches long. Make a scale on it by making a mark every ¼ inch. Halfway down the strip (at 2 inches), make a longer line to show the halfway mark. Tape this strip of paper to the bottle with the halfway mark at the same level as the water in the bottle.

You have made a water barometer. As the air pressure in the room increases, it will push down on the water in the bowl, forcing water into the bottle. You can see that the air pressure is high. If the air pressure is low, the bowl's water will rise, the bottle's water will sink, and you'll get a low pressure reading.

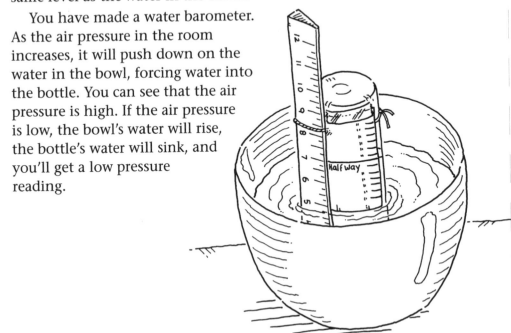

COMPOST SCULPTURES

*These decorative bags make interesting lawn sculptures,
and you'll end up with some handy compost in the spring!*

**WHAT YOU'LL
NEED**
Paper yard-waste
  bags
Crayons or perma-
  nent markers
String
Smaller brown paper
  bags
Twigs (optional)
Tape

You've probably seen those orange plastic bags that look like pumpkin faces and are filled with leaves. The ones you make will be even better for the environment. If you place them where they'll be protected during the winter, in a few months you'll have some compost in the bottom of the bags—just in time for your spring garden!

Before filling the yard-waste bags with leaves, decorate them with the crayons or markers. Animal faces, funny faces, or designs of any kind make interesting sculptures.

When finished, fill the bags with leaves. Tie the tops shut. You can add twigs for arms, use a smaller paper bag to make a hat—who knows where your imagination will take you!

SCIENTIFIC SIFTER

Archaeologists and other scientists often sift through sand, dirt, and other materials to find small artifacts and treasures. Make your own scientific sifter to find treasures.

WHAT YOU'LL NEED

Mesh onion or
  potato bag
Scissors
Cardboard
Ruler
Stapler and staples
Packing tape

Optional:
Magnifying glass
Notebook
Pencil
Reference books

Cut the metal clips off an onion bag, then cut the bag so you have a flat piece of mesh. Cut 2 rectangles out of cardboard that are the size of the mesh. Cut a matching hole in each piece of cardboard that is at least 2 inches smaller than the size of the mesh. Using 1 piece of cardboard, stretch the mesh over the hole and staple it in place. Take the second piece of cardboard and lay it on top (over the staples). (If you'd like to make an extra-fine sifter, use 2 or 3 pieces of mesh.) Tape the cardboard pieces together at the outside edges with packing tape.

Now it's time to go outside to explore! Sift through some dirt in your backyard, some sand at the beach, or some soil in the garden. (Of course, you need to ask permission before digging or sifting!) How many treasures can you come up with? Did you find living creatures (be sure to put them back after examining them), interesting rocks, shells?

Examine your findings with the magnifying glass, and then draw them in your notebook. Then you can sort, classify, and identify your treasures by comparing your drawings with pictures from reference books.

Mom will appreciate that you only bring pictures of your treasures into the house!

GYROCOPTER

This paper gyrocopter is just the thing to enjoy outside
on a warm spring day—or anytime it's not too windy or cold.

WHAT YOU'LL NEED

Paper
Ruler
Scissors or pinking
 shears
Paper clip

A "gyre" is a circular motion; a gyrocopter spins around when it flys. To explore gyre motion, make your own gyrocopter.

Cut out a 6½×1½-inch strip of paper. (Note: Using pinking shears will make the gyrocopter fly better, but ordinary scissors will work well too.) Starting at the top, cut a 3-inch slit down the middle of the strip to create a pair of wings. Fold the wings in opposite directions (see diagram). Attach a paper clip to the bottom of the strip for weight.

Drop the finished gyrocopter from an elevated spot, and watch it spin to the ground.

Now try experimenting. Make larger and smaller gyrocopters to see if size makes a difference when they fly. Think up other experiments you can try—make the wings longer, add 2 paper clips to the bottom.

Have gyrocopter races with friends who have made their own 'copters!

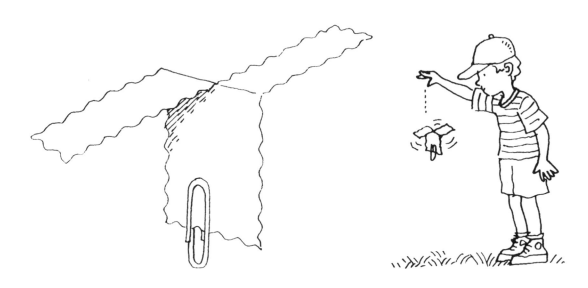

ARCTIC LIGHT

Watch how the reflective properties of ice cause this arctic light to give off a warm, welcoming glow on a winter night.

Adult Help Needed

WHAT YOU'LL NEED

Water
Large metal mixing bowl
Plastic yogurt container
Small stones or coins
Large tray with sides
Votive candle
Matches (adult use only!)

Pour a few inches of water into the mixing bowl. Fill the yogurt container with stones or coins, then center the container in the bowl. Slowly pour more water into the bowl so that it nearly reaches the rim of the smaller container. Place the bowl in the freezer until the water is frozen.

When frozen, remove the ice from the mold. If the ice doesn't come out easily, run warm water on the outside of the bowl and the ice should slip out. Then dump out the stones or coins from the yogurt container, and pour in warm water to loosen it. Remove the container, and place the ice candleholder on the tray.

Now it's time for sparkling fun. Place a votive candle in the opening, and have an adult light it. If you're fascinated by the way the light looks through the ice, go to your local library for some further study on light.

ASTROLABE

Learn how to measure the position of stars with
this simple instrument.

DIFFICULT

WHAT YOU'LL NEED

String
Ruler
Plastic protractor
Weight (washer,
    rock, or fishing
    weight)
Pen
Notebook
Flashlight (to see
    what you're
    writing)

When scientists describe the position of a star in the sky, they measure its position relative to the horizon. An instrument called an astrolabe measures how high above the horizon the star is in degrees. Here's how to make your own astrolabe.

Tie a 12-inch piece of string to the hole in the middle of the crossbar on the protractor. Tie a weight to the other end of the string. Hold the protractor so that the curved part is down and the 0 degree mark is closest to you. Sit on the ground, and look along the flat edge of the protractor with your eye at the zero mark. Point the flat edge at the star whose position you want to measure. Once you have the star at the end of your sight, hold the string against the side of the protractor.

Note the degree mark the string touches. Write this down in your notebook. This number tells you how many degrees above the horizon your star is.

Take readings for several stars. Return every 30 minutes and take new readings. Notice the pattern of the stars as they appear to move across the sky as the earth turns.

LEAF STENCILS

Leaves make lovely artwork—and unique greeting cards and stationery.

EASY

Adult Help Needed

WHAT YOU'LL NEED

Tempera paints
Water
Spray bottles
Leaves
Newspaper
White paper
Crayons (optional)

Make easy and safe spray paint by adding water to tempera paint to thin it. Then put the different colors of paint in different spray bottles.

Collect a variety of leaves with interesting shapes. Cover your work surface with newspaper. (The newspaper should be bigger than the paper you will be using so it will catch the "over spray" when you paint.) Put a few of the leaves you collected on a piece of paper.

Spray paint the leaves. (Be sure to spray around the leaves, too.) Let the paint dry, then take away the leaves. The image is called a stencil. You can also rub crayons along the edges of the leaves instead of using spray paint to create your stencil.

Make your leaf stencils into greeting cards, or make stationery by painting with light-colored paints. Overlap several leaves for an intricate design.

BE AN EAGER BEAVER

Beavers build their dens with mud and sticks. Build a miniature beaver den from common items.

WHAT YOU'LL NEED

Toothpicks or twigs
Modeling clay
Shoe box
Rocks
Leaves
Shallow saucer
Small plastic cup
Scissors

Use your hands to mix the toothpicks or twigs into the clay. (Be careful not to poke yourself!) Shape the clay into a den (like a small cave) with an opening.

To make a beaver habitat, get a large shoe box or other shallow box. (If you use a shoe box, you may want to cut down the sides.) At one end of the box, pile up some more clay, and place the beaver den on it. Place more clay, small rocks, leaves, and twigs over the bottom of the box.

Beavers build tunnels from their dens into nearby ponds. Put a small, shallow container in the bottom of the shoe box as a pond. (A small saucer that goes under a flower pot makes a good pond.) Use a small plastic cup as your tunnel. Cut the bottom out of the cup. Put the bottom of the cup into the den opening and the top of the cup by the pond. Use clay to attach the cup to the den and to cover the top of the cup so it looks like a tunnel.

This model shows the ingenious home design of beavers. They scurry down to the pond to get water and plants for dinner, then go back home without ever venturing outside where predators might see them.

Now the challenge is yours—what other kinds of animal homes can you make? Do some research in the library, collect your craft supplies, and build!

CHANGING COLORS

Experiment with *color filters*—you'll find that they let through
light the same *color* as themselves.

WHAT YOU'LL
NEED
Cardboard
Scissors
Ruler
Cellophane in red,
    blue, green,
    yellow, and
    orange
Tape
Markers
White paper

Take 5 pieces of 9×12-inch cardboard, and cut out the centers, leaving a frame that is 1½ inches wide all around. Using tape, securely fasten 1 sheet of colored cellophane to each cardboard frame. You have created 5 color filters.

Look through one of the filters. What does it do to the colors of objects in the room? Try another. Look through 2 filters at a time. What do you see?

Draw simple pictures of shapes on several pieces of white paper, using only 1 color marker for each piece of paper. View each picture through a filter that is the same color as the picture. What do you see? Look at the pictures through filters of different colors.

Continue to experiment with your filters.

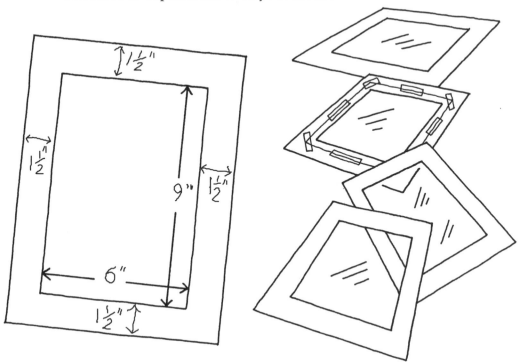

PIPE CLEANER BACKBONES

Use sculpture to learn that some animals have backbones that run through the center of their bodies, just like humans!

Use chenille stems to make skeletons of different animals. Start each skeleton by forming the backbone of the animal. Cut and bend the chenille stems to make other bone parts (legs, heads, tails). Try to make a dog first. Then make other creatures, such as birds, dinosaurs, fish, or reptiles. You might want to try a giraffe or a human. Use pictures of the animals as a guide if that will help you.

PATTERNED BUTTERFLIES

These beautiful butterflies look like they're made from stained glass! Study the patterns on real butterflies (from books or by looking at butterflies in your yard or garden), and see if you can re-create some of those patterns.

Study some reference books about butterflies to decide which butterfly you want to create. Draw a butterfly outline on the large sheet of paper. Tear the colored tissue into 3-inch shapes. Place a sheet of waxed paper over the butterfly outline. Use the liquid starch to paint tissue pieces onto the wax paper, filling in the outline of the butterfly with a mosaic of different colors.

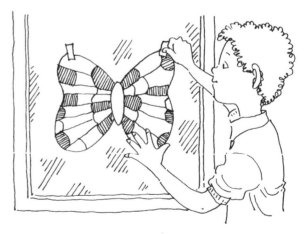

Add 1 or 2 more layers of tissue, and allow your butterfly to dry overnight. Cut out the butterfly, following the outline on the underlying paper. Slowly peel the tissue-paper butterfly off the waxed paper. Tape your butterfly to the window, and let the sun shine through!

FLYING FISH

Fish seem to fly through the air with this attractive mobile.

WHAT YOU'LL  **NEED**
Reference books
6 sheets of paper
Pencil
Scissors
Paper clips
Stapler
Newspaper
Paints
Paintbrush
Hole punch
String
Coat hanger

Find reference books about fish in your local library. There are many differently colored and shaped fish in the world. Find your favorite in the books, and make a fish mobile that will be sure to catch everyone's attention!

Draw the outline of the fish you have chosen, making sure the outline is about 7 inches long and at least 5 inches high. If you'd really like to go all out, choose 3 different fish and make a large outline shape for each. Trace your initial outline on 5 more sheets of paper—making a total of 6 fish. (If you are making 3 different fish, copy each outline once more—making a total of 2 outlines for each fish.) Use paper clips to hold the 2 fish shapes together, then staple them together at the edges. Staple all around the body except the back of the tail. Make a total of 3 fish this way.

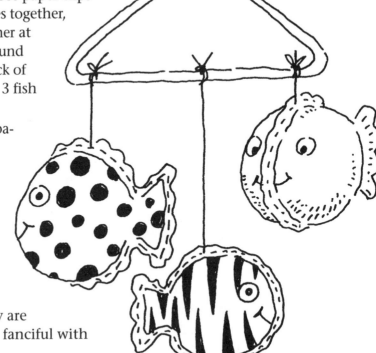

Tear sheets of newspaper into thin strips. Scrunch up the strips, and stuff them into the fish. When each fish is full, staple across the tail to keep the stuffing inside. Paint the fish anyway you like. You can paint them so they are realistic, or you can be fanciful with your painting!

Punch a hole in the top of each fish. Cut 3 lengths of string. Tie an end of a piece of string to the top of the fish, and then tie the other end of the string to a coat hanger. Repeat for the other 2 fish. Hang your fish mobile for all to see!

If you don't like fish, why not try a bird, dog, cat, or bear mobile. Your local library has all the books you need to do research on any of these animals!

NEIGHBORHOOD BIRD BATH

Birds love taking a bath during the summer. Make a bathtub just for them, and have the cleanest birds in the neighborhood!

MEDIUM

Adult Help Needed

WHAT YOU'LL NEED
Plastic milk jug
Heavy-duty scissors
Sand or a brick
Shallow plastic bowl
Water
Small rocks

First make the pedestal base for the bird bath out of a gallon milk jug. Have an adult slice off and cut curves into the top of the plastic milk jug. The curves should allow the shallow plastic bowl to sit securely on the milk jug. Put enough sand or a brick in the bottom of the milk jug to keep it from toppling over. Place the bowl on the jug-pedestal, and fill the bowl with water and a layer of small rocks. Then wait for the birds to come take a dip in their new tub. Don't be surprised if neighborhood cats, squirrels, rabbits, or other wildlife also love this backyard addition!

ARCTIC SNOW GOGGLES

Make your own Arctic Snow Goggles with some everyday cardboard.

MEDIUM

Adult Help Needed

WHAT YOU'LL
👓 NEED 👓

Cardboard
Pencil
Heavy-duty scissors
Craft or utility knife
    (adult use only)
Hole punch
String
Markers or colored
    pencils

Snow-covered areas are very bright places, even though they are very cold. That's because the sun's rays reflect off the snow. Those reflections can damage a person's eyesight. To protect their eyes from these harmful rays, the Inuit (native people of Canada, Alaska, and Greenland) wore goggles that they carved from wood or whalebone.

To make your own pair of snow goggles, draw an hourglass shape on the piece of cardboard. Be sure the shape is large enough to fit on the front of your face. Cut out the shape. Have an adult mark slits on the cardboard where your eyes are. (You hold the cardboard on your face, and the adult can mark the cardboard.) Have the adult use a craft or utility knife to cut out narrow eye slits. Punch holes in the upper corners of the goggles. Cut two 18-inch pieces of string. Feed an end of a piece of string through the hole on the side of the goggles, and tie a knot. Repeat for the other piece of string and the other hole.

Add a decorative border along the edges of your goggles with markers or colored pencils. Try out your goggles!

(**Warning**: These glasses reduce the glare of the sunlight reflecting off the snow—they are not protection from the sun! Never look directly at the sun, even with these goggles on! You could damage your eyes.)

Music Mania

Music makes the world go 'round—so start making some noise! There are so many ways that music affects our lives. It can make us happy, make us want to dance, help teach us our alphabet, and more. Add lots of music to your life—make great instruments, explore rhythms and sounds, perform for your family. You'll find all that and more in this chapter.

AIR GUITAR PLUS

Playing a rock star has never been easier...or more fun.

WHAT YOU'LL NEED
- Cardboard appliance box
- Pencil
- Scissors
- Glue
- Tempera paints
- Paintbrush
- Metallic felt-tip marker
- Straight pin
- Fishing line
- Duct tape

Who hasn't dreamed of being a rock star—a singing sensation dancing across videos and music lovers' hearts. This fun cardboard guitar can make pretending fun. It's like playing air guitar—with a little more than air to wrap your fingers around.

Draw a life-size guitar on the long end of an appliance box. You can make an acoustic guitar or an electric guitar shape. Trace around the neck of the guitar on cardboard to make another neck; make this one a bit longer than the original. Cut both pieces out, and glue the second neck to the back of the first neck. This will reinforce your guitar so you can strum wildly! If you've made an acoustic guitar, cut out a hole in the body of the guitar, so it looks like a real guitar.

Paint your guitar however you'd like. You can add your band's name, logo, or whatever you want. Try some psychedelic colors! When the paint is dry, draw frets (the lines along the neck of the guitar) with the metallic felt-tip marker.

With a straight pin, make 4 small holes for an electric guitar or 6 small holes for an acoustic guitar along the top of the neck and 4 or 6 holes at the bottom third of the body of the guitar. Measure the length from the top holes to the bottom holes, and add 4 inches. Cut 4 or 6 pieces of fishing line that length. Thread a piece of fishing line through the front of a top hole, and tape the line down on the back of the guitar with duct tape; repeat for the bottom hole. Do the same with the other holes and other pieces of line.

Now you're ready to jam—turn on the radio and play along!

CAN-CAN

Can you keep the beat? Sure you can-can!

WHAT YOU'LL NEED

3 small metal coffee cans with lids
White paper
Colored markers
Old magazines
Scissors
Glue
Measuring cup
Uncooked pinto beans
Unpopped popcorn
Uncooked rice
Heavy-duty tape

The magic of music is not just in the tune; it's in the rhythm. This coffee can trio of rhythm instruments can help you play along with any of your favorite songs.

Wash and dry the coffee cans. Decorate 3 sheets of paper with colorful drawings of musical notes or fun shapes. You can also use old magazines to cut out pictures of your favorite musical legends or stars, and glue them on the paper. Glue your design to the outside of the coffee can, covering the brand name and logo.

Now put ½ cup of uncooked pinto beans in a can, ½ cup of uncooked popcorn in another, and ½ cup of uncooked rice in the third. Pop on the plastic lids, and make sure they are securely in place. Tape the lids in place with heavy-duty tape.

Now it's time to shake, shake, shake your way to musical adventure. Notice how different the sounds inside each can are, thanks to the different shapes and densities of the content.

FISH LINE MUSIC

Make your own instrument that can be strummed!

DIFFICULT

Adult Help Needed

WHAT YOU'LL NEED

Smooth board,
 16×6×1 inches
Pencil
Ruler
Hammer
Ten 1-inch nails
Scissors
Nylon fishing line

Lay a 16×6×1-inch board flat on the table in front of you so that one of the 6-inch sides is nearest you. Draw 5 straight pencil lines down the length of the board about 1 inch apart, beginning 1 inch down from the top and 1 inch in from the left side. Pound a nail about ½ inch deep at the top of each line.

Cut 5 pieces of nylon fishing line in the following lengths: 14, 12, 10, 8, and 6 inches. Tie a loose slip knot in both ends of each piece of fishing line. Put the slip knot of the 14-inch piece of fishing line over the top left nail on your board, and pull the knot tight. Put the slip knot at the other end of the fishing line over a loose nail, and stretch the line as tightly as you can toward the bottom of the leftmost pencil line that you drew. Hammer the nail into the board about ½ inch deep. Nail the other pieces of fishing line onto the board in the same way. Work from left to right on the board, each time using the longest piece of fishing line that you have left.

You now have a musical instrument. Pluck each string with your index finger. Which string has the highest sound? Which has the lowest? Practice with your new instrument, and use it to make music.

FLOWERPOT BELLS

These clay bells ring true, inside or out.

MEDIUM

WHAT YOU'LL
👀 NEED 👀

Newspaper
Small clay flower-
    pots
Acrylic paint
Paintbrush
Clappers (small,
    wooden curtain
    rings; wooden
    beads; or other
    solid objects)
Thick string or twine
Coat hanger
Chopstick
Plastic mallet

Whether you ring these inside or hang them outside as chimes, these hand-painted bells will be music to your ears!

Cover your work surface with newspaper. Paint designs on your clay pot with acrylic paints . . . anything goes. This is your chance to be creative. Once the paint dries, tie 1 or 2 small, wooden curtain rings or a bead to a string to make the bell clapper—the object that strikes the inside of the bell to make it ring. Slip the end of the string through the hole in the bottom of the clay pot so the clapper dangles inside the bell. Don't forget to knot the string on the inside of the clay pot to hold the clapper in place.

Make a few bells, with different clappers, and tie them all to the bottom of a coat hanger so they don't touch. Hang the coat hanger, and play your bells! Experiment with tapping the bells with your fingers, a wooden chopstick, and a plastic mallet to find out what makes the best sound.

Chime away!

Percussion Fun
What do bells have in common with drums and xylophones? All three are percussion instruments; they must be hit to produce a sound. But not all bells have clappers. Wooden bells, such as the Chinese Temple Block, are clapperless—that is, you strike them on the outside with a hammer or rod.

PIE PAN TAMBOURINE

Ring in some fun with this musical craft.

Adult Help Needed

WHAT YOU'LL NEED

Foil pie pan
Nail
File or hammer
Jingle bells
Yarn or string

If keeping time to the music is your favorite pastime, check out this easy-to-make pie pan tambourine.

Punch holes in the edges of an aluminum foil pie pan with a nail. Have an adult help you smooth the sharp edges of the holes with a file or hammer. At each hole, tie a small jingle bell to the pan with yarn or string.

Now jingle those bells—you'll have a rhythmic adventure you won't be able to resist.

GLASS JAR JINGLE

Who knew water could help make music?

WHAT YOU'LL NEED

6 to 8 different-size glass jars with lids
Water
Metal fork

Gather together 6 to 8 different-size glass jars with lids. Fill each jar half full of cool water, and tightly close the lids. Use a metal fork to gently strike the jars. Can you hear the music ring? Do all the jars sound the same? Does the music change when you strike the top, middle, or bottom of the jar? Pour out half the water in each jar, and repeat the experiment. How have the tones changed? Once you're familiar with what note each of your jars will play when softly hit, you can try to play your favorite tunes.

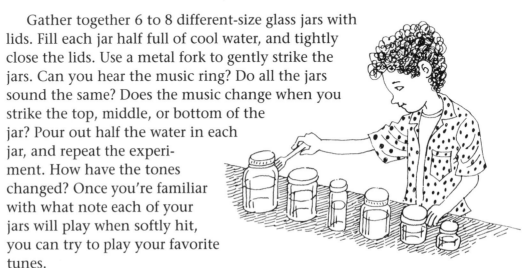

ANIMAL SOUNDS

You can create animal sounds just by varying the vibrations on this simple instrument!

WHAT YOU'LL NEED
1-quart milk carton
Scissors
String
Paper towel
Water

Cut the top off of a 1-quart milk carton, 4 inches from the bottom. Using scissors, punch a small hole in the center bottom of the carton, and thread the end of a 24-inch piece of strong string through the hole. On the outside of the carton, tie a knot that will not pull through the hole.

Wet a paper towel, squeezing out the excess water. Hold the milk carton with one hand. With your other hand, put the wet paper towel around the string about 10 inches from the carton. Give the wet towel a quick pull while pressing it with your fingers. It will make a squawking noise that is amplified by the milk carton.

By varying how much string you leave between the wet towel and the box, you can produce sounds resembling a rooster's crow and a lion's roar.

DISTINCTIVE DRUM

Drum up some distinctive fun.

WHAT YOU'LL NEED

Clean, round oat-
 meal box
Newspaper
Paints
Paintbrush
Construction paper
Scissors
Feathers or charms
Glue
Plastic wrap
Rubber band
Wooden spoons or
 other kitchen
 utensils
Rags (optional)

Make a drum that reflects who you are.

Clean out a small, round oatmeal box. Now you're going to decorate it with things you like or that are important to you. Cover your work surface with newspaper. You could paint your drum, glue construction paper cutouts on it, and glue on feathers and charms—just express yourself!

Next, wrap the open end of the can or box with at least 2 layers of clear plastic wrap. Use a very tight rubber band to hold the plastic wrap in place. Wooden spoons or kitchen utensils make great drumsticks to bang out a rhythm—but not TOO hard. You don't want to break the plastic wrap drumhead. If the drum is too loud, you can put a few rags inside to soften the tone.

Now drum to express the musical side of you!

Ear-Splitting Drum

The bodhran is a distinctive one-sided drum often used in Irish music. It gets its name from the Irish word for "deafener," because it can sound too loud when it is not played properly!

CHEERFUL CHIMES

Nail down some delicate notes.

EASY

WHAT YOU'LL NEED

6-inch block of wood
Sandpaper (optional)
Paint
Paintbrush
Markers
Stickers
Cord or yarn
Scissors
Different-size nails
Metal dowel

Find a long, flat block of wood that is about 6 inches long. Use sandpaper to smooth the wood if needed.

Paint or decorate the wood with markers and stickers. Cut 8 to 10 pieces of cord or yarn, each about 12 inches long. Tie a piece of cord or yarn every ½ inch along the block of wood. Trim the ends of all the cords so they are even. Tie the different-size nails on the dangling ends of the cord. Cut another length of cord for a hanger, and tie each end to an end of the block of wood.

Hang your chime from a porch or window. Stroke the dangling nails with a metal dowel for a lovely, tinkling sound. And when you're not playing your chimes, the wind will make beautiful music for you!

Triangular Tunes

For a cheerful sound, try playing a triangle. This simple instrument is made of a steel rod in the shape of a triangle open at one of its angles. It is usually hung by a cord and struck with a metal beater. And you thought triangles were just for math class!

BOTTLE CAP CLINKERS

Shake some bottle caps for fun and rhythmic beauty.

MEDIUM+

Adult Help Needed

WHAT YOU'LL NEED

Soda or beverage bottle caps
1 large nail (larger than a 2-inch nail)
Hammer
2-inch nails with large heads
Long piece of wood
Sandpaper (optional)

This clinking rattle will bring a whole new sound to your life. Collect dozens of bottle caps from old-fashioned glass soda or beverage bottles. With adult help, use the biggest nail to punch a hole through the center of each cap. Once each cap has a hole, place 4 caps on each 2-inch nail. Make between 4 and 10 nails with caps on them. Hammer the nails halfway into the wood, leaving the bottle caps free to jingle. (If the wood is rough, use the sandpaper to smooth it before hammering nails into it.) Shake the finished rattle for a distinctive sound. Shake, shake, shake it!

A Different Kind of Rattle

Did you know that some Native American Indians use rattles made from deer hooves attached to a long stick? These rattles are used along with traditional chants and dances at the tribe's ceremonial celebrations.

NATURE'S ORCHESTRA

You and your friends can strike up the band with these musical
instruments made from natural materials.

With a group of friends, collect rocks,
gravel, sand, sticks, shells, and anything
else from nature that you can use to
make musical instruments. Use your
imagination! (Don't harm live plants or
disturb animals in their habitats during
this project.) Put rocks in cans to shake.
Use sticks as drumsticks. Make a drum
from a hollow log or bark. After everyone
has an instrument, make beautiful
music together!

HUM ALONG WITH ME!

This humming instrument is sure to please!

Cut a circle of waxed paper that is 2 inches larger than
the top of a foil pie pan. Place the circle on top of the
pan, and press the excess paper down over the sides of
the pan. Tape the paper onto the pan at 2 opposite
points only. To play, place your lips lightly against any
edge of this instrument. Hum a tune, and watch the
paper vibrate to amplify the sound.

CLAP OUT A RHYTHM

Songs are more than music...clap out a rhythm to find out how.

WHAT YOU'LL NEED

Paper
Pencils

We all know songs are a series of notes strung together. But have you ever thought about the unusual rhythms of each song? This activity will help you understand them. Pick a simple song, such as "Mary Had a Little Lamb." Now clap out the song as you sing it aloud. Write the words on a piece of paper. Now mark the rhythms, using a straight up and down stroke for a short note and a long sideways stroke for a long note. Experiment with other songs; try something more complicated—how about your favorite bopper's latest hit. See if you and a friend can guess which song the other is clapping out!

PLASTIC WRAP RAP

Music is in the ear of the beholder.

WHAT YOU'LL NEED

Plastic wrap from various containers (candy, CD's, toys, etc.)

Have you ever made music with a piece of plastic pressed to your lips? If not, it's about time you did. Take a piece of plastic wrap from a candy box, CD, or shrink-wrapped toy, and hold it tightly between your fingers. Hold the edge of the plastic just below your lips, and blow across it until the plastic whistles. If it doesn't work at first, don't give up. Keep twisting the edge of the plastic toward or away from your lips as you blow until you hear a shrill, almost birdlike squeal. Now try another type of plastic, and keep trying others that are different sizes, thicknesses, and lengths. Do they make the same tones? Gather some friends for a plastic wrap band. It's music of a whole other kind.

WACKY WASHBOARD

Make a cardboard washboard for a musical treat.

MEDIUM

WHAT YOU'LL NEED

Corrugated cardboard box
Pencil
Heavy-duty scissors
Paint
Paintbrush
Glue

The washboard is a scratch-and-thump rhythm instrument that is a special favorite for those who play down-home music. Now you can make a cardboard duplicate.

Using illustration 2 as a guide, draw 2 washboard shapes on the side panel of a large corrugated cardboard box. Make sure you draw and cut out rectangular holes at the top of the instrument. Cut out the washboards, and paint one. On the unpainted washboard, peel off the top layer of paper to expose the corrugated ridges. Glue this to the unpainted side of the other washboard. Let the glue dry completely.

It's time to make music. Rake your fingers across the bumpy surface to create a fun, scratchy sound.

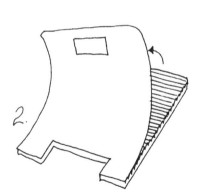

Banjo Buddy

The banjo is also a favorite of those who play down-home music. Brought to America from West Africa, where it was called a bania, the banjo is used as both a rhythm and solo instrument. A banjo and washboard duet makes for great country music fun!

WOOD TAP TURN ON

Tap, tap, tap on wood for a "tone" of fun.

WHAT YOU'LL NEED

6 to 8 different-size and -shape wood pieces
Small hammer
Tape recorder (optional)

Do all wooden doors produce the same knock? Do all blocks of wood sound the same when they are rapped and tapped on? Do they sound identical to the doors? Of course not. So gather up 6 to 8 wood pieces that are different sizes, shapes, and colors. Tap twice on the first block of wood with your hammer. Listen carefully so you'll remember the tone. Tap on the second. Then the third, and continue until you've tapped on all the blocks. Line up the blocks in musical order (highest-pitched tap to the right, lowest-pitched tap to the left). Now "play" your wooden block instrument for a remarkable sound. For added fun, tape record your songs!

JINGLE BELL PARADE

Turn your body into a musical instrument with jingle bells you can wear as a bracelet.

WHAT YOU'LL NEED

Grosgrain ribbon or bias tape
Measuring tape
Scissors
6 jingle bells
Needle
Thread
2 sets of snaps

Measure and cut the ribbon or bias tape into two 8-inch lengths. Evenly space 3 jingle bells on a piece of ribbon or bias tape. Sew the jingle bells on, and sew a snap on each end of the ribbon (half of the snap will be on one end of the ribbon, the other half will be on the other end of the ribbon). Repeat the process with the other jingle bells, the other snap, and the other piece of ribbon. You've made 2 bracelets. Snap a bracelet around each wrist. Once you've put the bracelets on, shake your arms to make some music. If you want, make jingle bell bracelets for your ankles, too. Listen to them jingle when you march with the band.

MUSICAL HISTORY

Discover your own musical roots.

EASY

WHAT YOU'LL NEED
Pad of paper
Pencil
Tape recorder

In today's hustle and bustle, look-to-the-future world, we often forget to look back. Take time to explore your musical past by following these simple instructions.

Ask your parents who your oldest relatives are. Ask if you can visit, write, or e-mail them to ask about the family's musical history. Did grandma play the piano? Did Great-Great-Aunt Minnie buy an organ from a traveling salesman in a covered wagon on the plains? Who were the family singers, and who couldn't carry a tune? If your family emigrated to the United States, do your relatives know or remember songs from the "old country"? If they do, be sure to have your relatives sing them so you can record them!

These recordings will be priceless treasures when you're older and have kids of your own to share them with. Be sure to take notes as you talk to these people. Once you start asking questions, you'll probably find out so much more about your family than just its musical history.

Bird Flute

Scientists have discovered the oldest playable musical instrument in the world. It's a flute carved from a bird's wing bone, made more than 9,000 years ago. The flute was discovered with other flutes at an ancient burial site in China.

MIX UP MUSIC

If you mix one song with another, can a third song be far behind?

If you've ever jumped from radio station to radio station in search of a better tune, you know how much fun this game can be. Turn your radio to the first available familiar tune, and write down the first phrase you hear. Now turn to the next station, and write down the second phrase. Go to the next station, and the next, until you have 6 phrases. When you're done, read the phrases as a new song. Now try to sing it! Did you wind up with a third song that's fun? I'll bet you did!

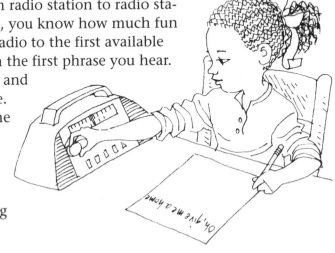

MAKE IT SNAPPY

*Is your favorite song too much fun to keep to yourself?
Then get snapping!*

Is it impossible to sit still when your favorite song comes on the radio? Then go with the flow, and snap your fingers to the beat. See if you can pick up the main line of the song and snap with every beat and syllable. Now try it double-time. See if you can cut that rhythm in half. This is a fun exercise in rhythm and a great way to participate in the song!

KOOL KAZOO

You don't need years of practice to make beautiful music.
All you need is this kazoo and a good song to hum.

WHAT YOU'LL NEED
Paper towel tube
Markers
Waxed paper
Rubber band
Scissors

Decorate the paper towel tube with markers. Wrap a piece of waxed paper over 1 end of the tube. Secure the waxed paper with a rubber band. Carefully cut 2 holes in the tube. To play your kazoo, hum your favorite song into the open end of the tube. To make other interesting sounds, make more kazoos with tubes that have different diameters, thicknesses, and lengths.

MARACA MUSIC

Keep the beat colorful and lively with these
multicolored maracas.

WHAT YOU'LL NEED
Small screwdriver
2 clear stiff plastic cups
Colored tape
Colorful pencil
Medium-size colored beads
Ribbon (optional)

Have an adult help you use the screwdriver to poke a pencil-size hole in the bottom of 1 of the plastic cups. Wind colored tape around the pencil to make a candy-cane striped pattern. Slide the pencil into the hole you just made. Wind more colored tape thickly around the pencil to hold it in place. Fill the cup with an assortment of colored beads, and place the other cup rim-to-rim with the first cup to make a closed container. Tape the cups together with colored tape. If you'd like, tie a ribbon around the pencil where it meets the cup's bottom to make pretty streamers. Now you can create a maraca beat that you and your friends can boogie to!

INSTRUMENT SAFARI

How often do you see signs of music in everyday life?

WHAT YOU'LL NEED

Old magazines
3-minute timer
Scissors
Paper
Glue

Does music influence our everyday lives? Of course it does. But this fun game will help you see just how often it pops up in the magazines you read—and how much you know about it when it does.

You can play this game by yourself or with friends. Get permission to rip apart some old magazines, and set them beside you. Set a timer for 3 minutes—or use an egg timer. See how many signs of music (instruments, notes, song titles, music reviews) you can find, and cut or tear them out. Get 1 point for each sign of music you cut out. For bonus points, name the instruments or sing the songs you've found.

Now for the creative part, make a collage with all your musical finds to remind you that music is part of your life!

Elephant Instruments

Did you know that elephants often communicate at sound levels as low as 5Hz? So if you were ever to go on a real safari and you were to flap your hands back and forth very quickly, faster than five times a second, an elephant will be able to hear the tone produced. To the elephant, your flapping hands are an interesting safari instrument!

MATHEMATICAL MAGIC

Exploring the world of numbers has never been so much fun! In this chapter, you'll find many games and activities, and you'll be surprised when you find they are all about using and increasing your math skills. Numbers are all around us, from telling time to comparing prices when you are shopping at the mall. Since math is so important, have fun with it!

ONE TO TEN

Create a one-to-ten book, and illustrate it with *one-to-ten pictures*.

WHAT YOU'LL NEED
11 pieces of paper
Stapler
Crayons or markers

To make the book, staple together 11 pieces of paper (the top sheet is the cover). Write a title on the cover, and then number each of the following spreads (the 2 pages that face each other) with the numbers 1 through 10. On each spread, draw a picture that corresponds to the number on the page. On spread 1, draw 1 thing. On spread 2, draw 2 items. On spread 3, draw 3 things, and so on. Create a theme for your book. For example, make a 1-to-10 book of animals, and choose a different animal for each spread (1 bear, 2 cats, 3 zebras, etc.). Or illustrate the numbers with facts about yourself. For instance, on the "1" spread, draw something you have 1 of (1 heart, 1 dog, or 1 toothbrush). On the "2" spread, draw something you have 2 of (2 feet, 2 hands, or 2 cats). Keep going!

SUPER-STRONG EGGSHELLS

Arches (even ones made of eggshells) are strong because they exert horizontal as well as vertical force to resist the pressure of heavy loads. Don't believe me? Try it for yourself.

WHAT YOU'LL NEED
4 eggs
Transparent tape
Scissors
Telephone books

Carefully break off the small end of the 4 eggs, and pour out the insides (after getting adult permission, of course). Wind a piece of transparent tape around the center of each eggshell. Cut through the center of the tape to make 4 dome-shaped shells. Throw away the broken end of each shell. Lay the 4 domes on a table, cut sides down, arranged in the shape of a square. Now it's time to guess how many telephone books you can lay on top of the shells before they break. You'll be surprised!

CRAZY CHECKERBOARD

Make this checkerboard with any colors you like. Measure two colors of construction paper, and weave them together.

DIFFICULT

WHAT YOU'LL NEED

2 pieces of differently colored paper (1 piece 8×8 inches, 1 piece 8×10 inches)
Scissors
Ruler
Transparent tape
8×10-inch cardboard
Craft glue
Cardboard scraps
Markers

Fold the 8×10-inch sheet of paper in half, bringing the 8-inch sides together. Cut 7 slits, 1 inch apart, from the folded edge to within 1 inch of the other edge. Cut out eight 1-inch-wide strips from the 8×8-inch piece of paper. Unfold the first sheet of paper.

Weave the paper strips through the slits from left to right. Weave over and under the slits. If you started by weaving the first strip over the first slit, weave the second strip under the first slit, the third strip over the first slit, and so on. This will create a checkerboard.

When you have woven all 8 strips through the paper, make the ends of the strips even and straight. Carefully turn the checkerboard over. Place transparent tape along the left and right sides of the checkerboard to hold the strips in place. Turn the checkerboard right side up, and glue it to the cardboard.

Cut small circles out of cardboard, stack them 3 or 4 pieces high, and glue them together. Create enough for 2 sets of checkers. Make each set a different color. Now play checkers!

PIZZA TIC-TAC-TOE

Here's "food" that your parents won't yell at you for playing with!

MEDIUM

WHAT YOU'LL NEED

Cream felt
Scissors
Ruler
Red felt
Tan felt
20 inches of brown satin ribbon (1/8 inch wide)
Craft glue

Cut a 5-inch-diameter circle out of the cream felt. This is the crust. For the pepperoni game pieces, cut five 1-inch circles from the red felt. For the mushroom game pieces, cut five 1-inch squares from the tan felt. Trim the tan squares into mushroom shapes.

Cut the ribbon into four 5-inch lengths. Glue the 4 lengths of ribbon to the cream circle to make a tic-tac-toe grid. Trim the extra ribbon that hangs over the sides of the felt circle.

To play, place the pepperoni and mushroom game pieces within the squares on the grid—just as you would for a regular game of tic-tac-toe.

Now it's time to practice your strategy to achieve victory!

That's a Big Pizza Pie!

The 1995 *Guinness Book of World Records* lists the largest baked pizza on record as 37.4 meters in diameter—that's 12,159 square feet! This cheesy delight was baked in Norwood, South Africa, on December 8, 1990. By the way, 75 percent of Americans under 35 say they sometimes have pizza for breakfast.

INTERSECTING CIRCLES

Here's a handy way to think about sorting and categories.

WHAT YOU'LL NEED

Markers
Paper
Old magazines
Scissors
Craft glue

A Venn diagram is a diagram that demonstrates intersecting sets.

To make a Venn diagram, draw 2 overlapping circles on a piece of paper. Cut out pictures from an old magazine to sort into groups. You might choose 1 kind of picture to start with, such as pictures of animals, clothing, toys, etc. Think of 2 different qualities you could use for sorting the pictures in your group. For example, you could sort many of the animal pictures into 2 groups: animals with tails and animals with spots. Or you might try to sort clothing pictures into clothing with pockets and clothing with buttons.

Place 1 group of pictures in the first circle you've drawn and the other group in the other circle. Use the overlap section in the middle of the circles for pictures that fit both groups (animals that have tails and spots, clothing that has pockets and buttons). You've created a Venn diagram! Glue your pictures in place to complete the diagram.

You can also try drawing and illustrating your own invented categories instead of using magazine pictures, sorting canceled stamps into Venn diagrams, or making a 3-circle Venn diagram with 3 categories that overlap!

GIANT MAZE

*Create a maze, and challenge your friends
to get through it!*

WHAT YOU'LL NEED

Bristol board or
  light- to
  medium-weight
  cardboard
Pencil
Markers
Small-tipped black
  marker
Clear vinyl adhesive
  paper
Wax crayon
  (optional)

Use a pencil to draw a maze on a large piece of bristol board or light- to medium-weight cardboard. Draw the correct route through the maze (all the way to the exit) first. You might want to get ideas for drawing your maze from other mazes you find in coloring books or activity books. Start making other routes through the maze that look like they lead to the exit but only lead to dead ends.

Why not pick a theme for your maze, with traps and decorated dead ends. Use the markers to illustrate your theme. Is Roger running from the vampire? Is Sara searching for her sucker? After you've finished drawing and decorating the maze, go back over all the pencil lines with the small-tipped marker.

Cover the board with clear vinyl adhesive paper so your friends can try escaping from your maze again and again. (Have them use their fingers or a wax crayon, which can be wiped off.)

MINI MINIATURE BOWLING

Practice your math skills by keeping score of this fun game!

WHAT YOU'LL NEED

Black crayon
10 foam cups
Craft glue
2 pieces of card-
    board (approxi-
    mately 10 or
    more inches
    square)
Transparent tape
Black and red mark-
    ers
4 Ping-Pong balls
2 large books
Paper
Pencil

Use a black crayon to number the cups from 1 to 10 on the upper inside of each cup. Glue the cups to a piece of cardboard. Allow the glue to dry, then run a strip of tape around all the cups to hold them in place.

Color 2 Ping-Pong balls with the black marker and 2 balls with the red marker. Use a book to prop up your cardboard at a 45-degree angle so the 7 through 10 cups are at floor level and cup number 1 is raised. Make a ramp with the remaining cardboard, book, and tape. Tape one end of the cardboard on the floor, with the book underneath the other end to form a ramp. The angle of this ramp shouldn't be as steep as that of the cups, and the end of the ramp should be 5 to 7 inches away from the cups.

Each player takes a turn rolling the balls up the ramp and into the cups. After rolling 2 balls, a player adds up (the cup numbers are added) and writes down his or her score before the other player bowls. The player with the highest score wins.

MATH WAR

Make these cards in a flash! You'll have lots of fun with your friends as you get faster and faster at addition, subtraction, and even multiplication by playing this simple card game.

WHAT YOU'LL NEED

Package of plain index cards (any size, any color)
Colored markers

Use a marker to print a number from 1 to 12 on each card (write BIG). You can use the same number more than once. This will make things more fun as you play the game. Decorate the backs of the cards, if you'd like.

You'll need at least 2 players for Math War. The dealer gives each player a card until all the cards have been distributed evenly. To play, each person draws from the top of his pile and lays a card out, face up, on the table (just like in WAR with regular cards). The first person to yell out the correct sum of both numbers on the cards wins that round of play and takes the cards. The game continues until 1 person has all the cards.

Vary the game by changing from addition to subtraction problems, even multiplication!

HOW MANY SQUARES?

Figure out how many squares there really are on
a checkerboard!

DIFFICULT

**WHAT YOU'LL
NEED**
Checkerboard

This sounds easier than it is! You can easily see all the small squares on a checkerboard, but don't forget about all the other squares that are made by combining the small ones! Don't just count the small squares—count every square! That means each small square counts as 1 square. Each group of 4 squares becomes a bigger square, and is counted as 1 square. Each group of 16 squares becomes another square that is counted. Count them all! Try this one day and then on another day—did you come up with the same number of squares each time? Keep trying!

CEREAL GRAPH

These three-dimensional "graphs" are fun to make, and you
can see how easy it is to make a graph with objects
as well as numbers.

EASY

**WHAT YOU'LL
NEED**
Cereal with different colors or shapes
Large sheets of paper
Markers or colored pencils

Pour out a handful of cereal, and estimate (or guess) which color is the most common (no counting allowed). Arrange the cereal in rows according to color. Place the rows, side by side, onto a sheet of paper. Now look at the graph to see which color cereal was most common. Was your estimate correct? Will another handful produce the same results? Try the same project a few more times, and write down the results. The same graphing exercise can be done with snack crackers, sorting by shape. For a more challenging option, try a bag of assorted dried beans or a bag of pasta in different shapes or colors.

MANKALA COUNTING GAME

Kids the world over love counting games. This game from Africa is fun for kids of all ages.

WHAT YOU'LL NEED

Cardboard egg cartons
Scissors
Tape
Paints
Paintbrush
Small stones

Remove the lid from an egg carton, and tape an extra cup (cut from another carton) to each end. These end cups are used as banks, where players store their winnings. Use the paints and paintbrush to decorate your egg cups if you want, then let the paint dry.

Put 4 stones into each cup, but leave the banks empty. The first player starts the game by taking the stones from any cup. Beginning with the next cup and moving counterclockwise, he drops a stone into each cup. Next, he takes the stones from the cup into which his last stone fell. He continues emptying and depositing stones until his last stone falls into an empty cup. (The first turn is the only time a turn ends this way.)

The second player moves in the same direction, empties the cup of his choice, and redistributes the stones. If his last stone falls into a cup with 3 stones, he wins all the stones in that cup and places them in his bank. But if any stone other than the last one falls into a cup with 3 stones, the first player wins the stones from that cup. Players alternate turns until 4 or fewer stones are left in the carton. The player with the most stones wins.

TIC-TAC MATH

By adding a few numbers, you can turn an old game into something new!

Draw a normal tic-tac-toe board (2 lines down, 2 lines across). Instead of using Xs and Os, players take turns putting in a number between 1 and 9. The winner is the person who fills in a row so it adds up to 15! Numbers can only be used one time per game.

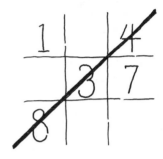

BRAINTEASER ART

Make a brainteaser for your friends to figure out, while creating wonderful art!

Use a stencil to create pictures out of geometric designs. Try a butterfly with lots of circles within circles or a house with squares for windows, shutters, chimneys, and even bricks. Keep track of the number of shapes you have drawn. If you want, use markers to make your brainteaser a kaleidoscope of color.

Be sure to count the shapes as you draw your picture, or you could end up teasing yourself!

When you're finished with your drawing, challenge a friend or family member to count the shapes.

SODA CAN SOCCER

This game involves lots of kicking, but it will also help you improve your addition skills if you keep score of all your points.

WHAT YOU'LL NEED

11 soda cans
Construction paper
Masking tape
Markers
Sand (for weighing down the cans)
Packing tape
Soccer ball
Paper
Pencil

Cover the sides of the cans with construction paper, and write point values on them: mark 1 on a single can, and mark 2 cans with the numbers 2, 3, 5, 7, and 10. Put a little sand in each can to keep them from blowing over. Cover the tops of the cans with packing tape.

In a flat, open area, set up the cans along a straight line. Spread the cans out a little. Place the cans in a straight line, putting the lower numbers in the center and the higher numbers toward the ends. Start from about 10 feet away, on a line with the center can, and call out and point to the cans you are aiming for. Kick the ball toward the cans. You'll only get points for the cans you called and hit. It doesn't count if you call out the 7 and hit the 3, for example.

Rotate with your friends, taking turns catching the ball, resetting the cans, and throwing the ball back for the next shooter. Also, have someone keep score, adding the hits until a player reaches 20 points.

GIGANTIC DOMINOES

These dominoes are big enough for a giant, but it doesn't take a giant to make them! All you need are foam trays and lots of colorful sticker dots. Use your math skills when you play the finished game.

MEDIUM

WHAT YOU'LL NEED
Foam food trays (from fruits or vegetables only)
Scissors
Pen
Ruler
Sticker dots

Wash and dry the foam trays. Make the trays into rectangles by cutting off the rounded corners. Measure and draw a line across the middle of each tray, from a long side to the other long side. Add round self-stick dots so the trays look like regular dominoes. (See a box of dominoes if you're unsure where to place the dots on the foam dominoes.) Now it's time for domino fun—start adding those dots together!

MATH POTATO

Play hot potato with numbers, but be careful not to get "burned"!

DIFFICULT

In the game Hot Potato, players toss a potato or beanbag around in a circle while music is playing. The person who is holding the potato when the music stops is out of the game. Math Potato is a little different. In this game, you toss math problems back and forth as fast as you can. Here's how it works.

The first player starts by making up a simple math problem, such as 5 + 3. The next player must "toss" it to someone else by solving the problem and making a new problem out of the solution. For example, Player 1 says, "5 plus 3 equals _____." Player 2 solves the problem by answering "8," then tosses it to Player 3 by saying, "8 minus 7 equals _____." Player 3 solves the problem,"1," then tosses it back to Player 1 by saying, "1 plus 13 equals _____," and so on. Players who give the wrong answers are out until the next game.

ANGULAR LOGIC

Capture as many triangles as you can corner!

**WHAT YOU'LL
NEED**
Paper
Pencil
Ruler

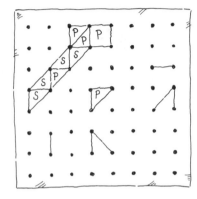

Make a grid of dots (8 across and 8 down makes a good game). Each player takes a turn by drawing 1 line that connects 2 dots. The object is to make the most triangles.

When you create a triangle, write the first letter of your name inside it so you can count each players' triangles later. When you create a triangle, you get to draw another line. Play until there are no more dots to connect. The player with the most triangles wins. (NOTE: Lines cannot cross each other.)

UPS AND DOWNS

Keep track of temperature changes, just like a real weather forecaster.

**WHAT YOU'LL
NEED**
Outdoor ther-
mometer
Paper
Pen

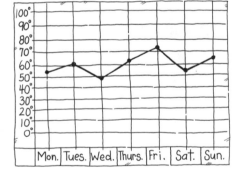

You can watch the news for your weather forecast. But now you can keep track of what the weather has been.

Put a thermometer outdoors—out of the sun—and check it at the same time each day. Record the daily temperatures. Make a graph of your temperature readings. Every week, connect the dots on the graph to make a line showing the temperature ups and downs. Which day was the coldest? Which was the warmest? Do you see a trend? Is it getting colder or warmer?

TREASURE MAP

It's fun to have your friends hunt for buried "treasure"
using a treasure map!

First you'll need some treasure to bury (just something you can hide—maybe some small toys). Hide the treasure in your yard someplace; you can bury it, put it in some bushes, or place it under a rock, etc. (If you are digging in your backyard, be sure to ask permission first!)

Use a piece of brown paper (part of a paper grocery bag will work) to create a map of your yard. The map will show where the treasure is hidden. Put a large X on the map where you hid the treasure. Include the number of paces (footsteps) from place to place (oak tree to large rock to gate to treasure), so you'll have to be good at both counting and writing directions.

Roll the map up, and tie it with twine so it looks like a real treasure map. Then give the map to a friend, and see if he or she can find the hidden treasure.

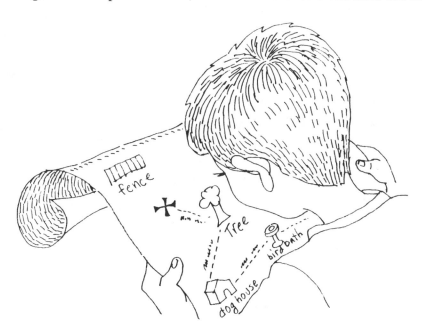

WHEEL OF TIME

What time is it in Sydney, Australia, right now? With this activity, you'll be able to tell the time all over the world.

DIFFICULT

WHAT YOU'LL NEED

Large piece of poster board
Scissors
Yardstick
Markers
Thumbtack
Large piece of cardboard

The world is divided into 24 time zones. When it's midnight in one time zone, it can be noon in another time zone—in fact, it can be two different days!

Cut a piece of poster board into a large circle. Draw lines that divide the circle into 24 equal-size wedge-shaped pieces. Write an hour of the day in each time zone. Start with 12 A.M., then 1 A.M., then 2 A.M., and so on. Be sure to continue through the P.M. times also, going in numerical order. Write the hours near the center of the circle. Put a thumbtack in the center of the circle, and attach the circle to a piece of cardboard larger than the circle. On the cardboard, mark sections that correspond to the hours on the poster board. Use the chart at right to write in the place names (be sure to write them in the exact order listed). Now you're ready to find out what time it is anywhere in the world.

1 A.M.	central Pacific Ocean
2 A.M.	Honolulu, Hawaii
3 A.M.	Anchorage, Alaska
4 A.M.	Los Angeles, California
5 A.M.	Denver, Colorado
6 A.M.	Chicago, Illinois
7 A.M.	New York, New York
8 A.M.	Caracas, Venezuela
9 A.M.	Rio de Janeiro, Brazil
10 A.M.	mid-Atlantic Ocean
11 A.M.	Atlantic Ocean
12 P.M.	London, England
1 P.M.	Paris, France
2 P.M.	Cairo, Egypt
3 P.M.	Moscow, Russia
4 P.M.	Dubai, United Arab Emirates
5 P.M.	Karachi, Pakistan
6 P.M.	Indian Ocean
7 P.M.	Bangkok, Thailand
8 P.M.	Beijing, China
9 P.M.	Tokyo, Japan
10 P.M.	Sydney, Australia
11 P.M.	western Pacific Ocean
12 A.M.	Auckland, New Zealand

Check your watch. What time is it where you are? Turn the circle until that time lines up with the name of the city in your time zone. When you line up your time, you can read your time-zone chart to tell you what time it is in London, Paris, Beijing, or Auckland! The world is at your fingertips!

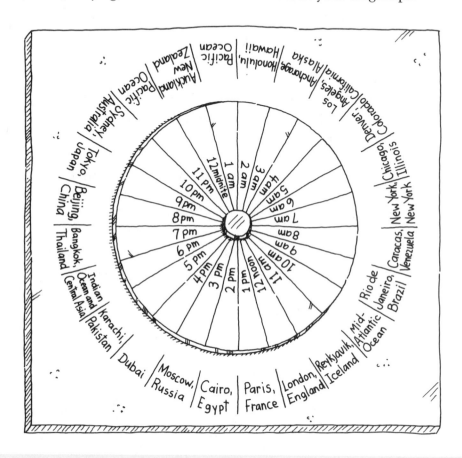

Is It Really Broken?

During the course of a day, how many times is a broken clock correct?
The answer is 48, once in each of the 24 time zones for A.M. and once in each of the 24 time zones for P.M.

REUSABLE CALENDAR

This calendar can be used again and again, since you simply turn the spools over to the correct month and day.

WHAT YOU'LL NEED

3 large spools
Paint
Paintbrush
Paper
Scissors
Markers
Craft glue
Transparent tape
2 pieces of wood or
    heavy cardboard
1 wooden dowel

Paint the spools, and let them dry. Cut out 3 paper strips, 1 to fit around the middle of each spool. Use a marker to print the months on the first strip; the numbers 1, 2, 3 on the second strip; and the numbers 0 to 9 on the third strip. Glue a strip to each spool.

Cut out 3 more strips that are slightly longer than the first 3. Cut out a window in each; the windows should be large enough to show the month and date on the first strips made. Place each strip over a spool, and tape the ends of each strip together. Be sure the sleeves move freely around the spools.

For the base, use 2 pieces of wood or cardboard that are the same size. Paint them however you want. Glue the dowel to the center of 1 piece of wood. When the paint and glue have dried completely, place the spools on the dowel. Place the month spool first, the spool with the numbers 1 through 3 next, and the spool with the numbers 0 throught 9 last. Glue the dowel to the middle of the other piece of wood. Let the glue dry completely.

Turn your spools to the correct month and day. Keeping track of the date was never so much fun!

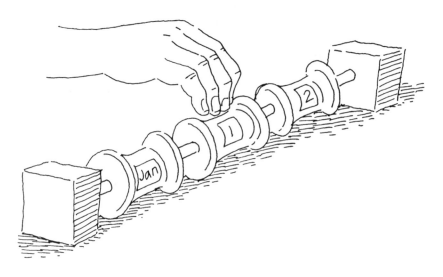

HOW TALL IS IT?

How can you measure the height of a tree when it's really tall?
Here's a neat trick to help you do it.

MEDIUM

WHAT YOU'LL NEED
Partner
Yardstick or tape measure
Pencil

You'll need a partner to do this activity. Use a yardstick to measure a straight line 60 feet from the tree you want to measure. Then have your partner stand there and hold the yardstick straight up with the bottom touching the ground. (A yardstick will work for trees that are up to about 30 feet tall. For very tall trees, you can do this activity with a metal tape measure instead of a yardstick.)

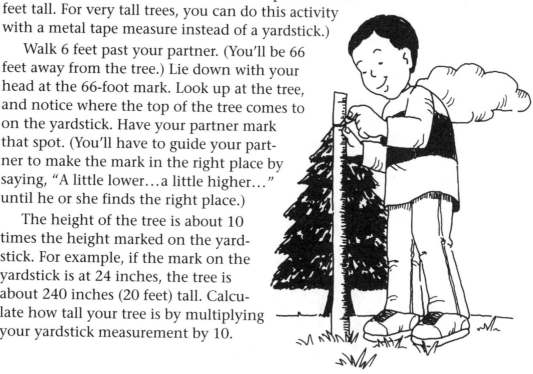

Walk 6 feet past your partner. (You'll be 66 feet away from the tree.) Lie down with your head at the 66-foot mark. Look up at the tree, and notice where the top of the tree comes to on the yardstick. Have your partner mark that spot. (You'll have to guide your partner to make the mark in the right place by saying, "A little lower…a little higher…" until he or she finds the right place.)

The height of the tree is about 10 times the height marked on the yardstick. For example, if the mark on the yardstick is at 24 inches, the tree is about 240 inches (20 feet) tall. Calculate how tall your tree is by multiplying your yardstick measurement by 10.

Tree Growth
A tree will grow differently in a windy climate than in a calm climate. If a strong wind usually blows from one direction, for example, the tree's trunk and branches will grow the way the wind pushes them.

FIND THE PRESENTS

*In this game of strategy, race your opponent
to locate the hidden presents.*

**WHAT YOU'LL
NEED**

Drawing paper
Ruler
Markers
Scissors
Construction paper
Pencils

To make the game board, draw an 8×8-inch square on a piece of drawing paper. Divide the square into 64 squares that are 1×1 inch. There will be 8 squares across and 8 squares down. Label the rows across A through H, and label the rows down 1 through 8 as shown. Take your original to a copy center, and make copies. You'll need 4 copies to play 1 game. (Save your original game board to make more copies for later games.)

On a piece of construction paper, draw 10 presents. Make four 1×2-inch presents and six 1×1-inch presents. Decorate your presents, and cut them out. Each player gets 2 large presents, 3 small ones, and 2 game boards.

To play the game, each player arranges their presents on 1 of their game boards. Then take turns guessing the location of your opponent's presents by calling out the name of the square. For example, you might ask if the present is in E-3. If the answer is no, mark the E-3 spot on your blank game board with an X; if the answer is yes, mark it with a star. Then your friend takes a turn. The first person to find all the presents wins.

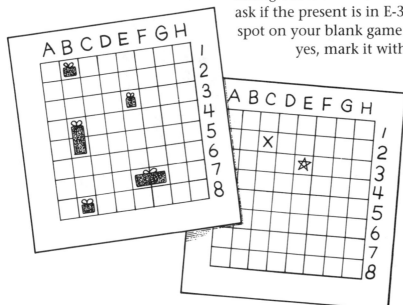

MAKE A TANGRAM

A tangram is like a recyclable puzzle, because you can make so many shapes and patterns with it.

DIFFICULT

WHAT YOU'LL NEED

8×8-inch sheet of light cardboard
Ruler
Scissors
Pencil

The Chinese call this puzzle *ch'i ch'iao t'u,* which means "ingenious puzzle with seven pieces." Seven geometric shapes make up the puzzle. Rearranged in different ways, these 7 pieces can make as many as 1,600 different designs.

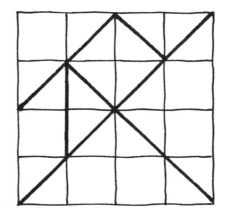

Look closely at the pattern in the accompanying picture. Use your ruler and pencil to draw an 8×8-inch square on the cardboard. The heavy black lines are the cutting lines. If you'd like, you can decorate your tangram—color each piece a different color, create different patterns on each one, or whatever you like. (NOTE: It is easier to color or decorate your tangram puzzle before you cut it apart.)

Try to re-create the design shown here. Then invent new shapes of your own. Trace the outside shape of your new designs, and challenge friends and family members to arrange the tangram pieces to match your designs.

A Favorite Author's Favorite Game

Lewis Carroll, the author of *Alice in Wonderland,* was a great fan of tangrams. He is said to have had a Chinese book made of tissue paper that had 323 tangram designs in it!

ROUND 'N' ROUND

This miniature Ferris wheel really works! Just carefully count and measure the materials, and be sure to ask an adult for help.

WHAT YOU'LL NEED

Cardboard
Pencil
Ruler
Scissors
Knitting needle
2 wooden or plastic thread spools
Glue
32 craft sticks
8 used wooden matchsticks
2 metal coat hangers
2×4-inch piece of wood cut 16 inches long
4-inch-long dowel (small enough to fit through hole in spool)
8 foam egg carton sections
Strong thread and needle
Stapler and staples
Markers
Glitter

Draw two 3-inch circles on the cardboard. Cut out the circles. Using the knitting needle, make a hole large enough for the dowel to fit through the center of each circle. Place a spool over the hole on each circle (make sure the holes in both circles line up), and trace around the spool.

Use a pencil and ruler to measure and divide each circle into 2, then 4, then 8 sections. Glue 8 craft sticks along the lines you have drawn. When these are dry, glue 8 more craft sticks to each circle along the edges between the first 8 sticks you glued on. First glue on 4 (leaving every other space unglued). When those are dry, glue on the other 4.

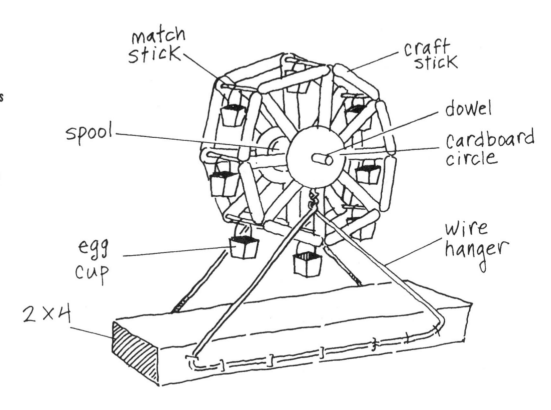

Turn 1 cardboard circle over, and glue the spool over the center hole. Wait for the glue to dry, then glue the second circle to the spool. Make sure the divided sections of each circle line up with the other circle.

Measure the distance between the 2 circles at 1 of the 8 divided sections. Cut 8 wooden matchsticks slightly longer than that length so they will fit tightly. Glue the matchsticks between the 2 craft sticks at each of the 8 sections. This is the wheel.

Bend the tops (hook parts) of 2 coat hangers into circles that are slightly larger than the dowel. Staple a hanger onto each side of the wooden base (make sure both hangers are the same height).

On cardboard, draw around the second spool 4 times. Cut out the 4 circles. Make a hole with the knitting needle in the center of each circle for the dowel. Push the dowel through a circle, the first hanger, another circle, the wheel's spool, another circle, the second hanger, and the last circle.

Attach each egg carton seat to the matchsticks with a needle and small piece of thread. Make sure the seats clear the base when the wheel turns. Decorate the Ferris wheel with markers, glue, and glitter.

That Was No Lightweight Wheel!

Did you know that the first Ferris wheel stood 264 feet high and had 36 cars that carried 60 passengers each—a total of 2,160 riders! This popular ride opened to the public in 1893; it weighed 1,200 tons and was powered by two 1,000 horsepower engines!

STRING SENSATION

Make elegant wall hangings by creating cool geometric shapes out of string.

DIFFICULT

Adult Help Needed

WHAT YOU'LL NEED

Large dinner plate
Paper
Pencil
Scissors
Large board (size you want your finished artwork)
Colored felt or paper (big enough to cover board)
Craft glue
8 glass-head map pins
String or embroidery floss
Pop-top (from soda can)
Thumbtack

Trace a large dinner plate onto paper to make a circle, then cut out the circle and fold it in half. Fold the circle in half again (into fourths), then again (into eighths). Unfold. Cover a large board by gluing down felt or paper, then place the paper circle in the center of the covered board with 1 fold going straight up and down (imagine folds are numbered 1 through 8, with 1 at the top).

Place a pin in the board at the end of every fold, next to the paper circle (the pins should be sticking up a little). Once all 8 pins are in place, remove the paper circle. Tie 1 end of the string or floss to pin number 1, and begin winding around the pins in the circle. Go from 1 to 2, 2 to 3, all the way around the circle—making a loop (but not a knot) around each pin. Keep string tight, but don't pull pins loose.

After you've looped all the pins in the circle, go around again in this order: 1-3-5-7-1-2-4-6-8. Go around the circle a last time, looping pins in this order: 2-5-8-3-6-1-4-7-2.

Make a knot when you get back to pin 2, and cut the string.

Hang your string art by attaching a pop-top from a soda can (be careful, it might be sharp!) to the back of the board with a thumbtack.

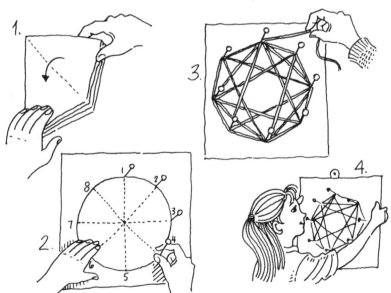

STARS AND STRIPES FOREVER

Create a red, white, and blue magnet that looks like a miniature U.S. flag. Then compare it to the real stars and stripes!

WHAT YOU'LL NEED

26 toothpicks
Red marker
Plastic lid
Craft glue
Scrap of blue construction paper
Ruler
Scissors
Tiny gold stars or glitter
Strip of sticky-backed magnet

Use the red marker to color 14 toothpicks. Arrange the toothpicks on the plastic lid, starting with 2 red toothpicks across the top, then 2 natural-colored toothpicks. Alternate 2 toothpicks of each color to create the stripes of the U.S. flag. Use glue to hold the toothpicks together. Don't add too much glue or the red color on the toothpicks will bleed.

Glue a 1-inch square of blue paper to the upper left corner of your flag. Cover the blue paper with a thin layer of glue, then sprinkle it with tiny stars or glitter. You probably won't fit 50 stars on this small flag, so just add as many as you can.

When your flag has dried completely, peel it from the lid. Trim any excess glue with scissors. Then stick a piece of sticky-backed magnet on the back of the flag. Hang your flag on the refrigerator for everyone to see!

After you've made the U.S. flag, which represents our country, create a flag that represents YOU. Use any colored markers you like, as well as different colored pieces of construction paper, glitter, stars, or other tiny decorations.

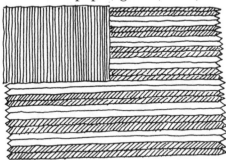

Long May She Wave

Here's a riddle to stump your friends: What is the one place where the American flag flies 24 hours a day, is never raised or lowered, and is never saluted?
Answer: The Moon!

MULTIPLY THE FUN!

EASY

WHAT YOU'LL NEED

Manila file folders
Colorful markers
Index cards
Clear vinyl adhesive paper
Small toys or coins
Die

It's easy and fun to make these simple math games with file folders and colorful markers. Cover them with clear paper, and they'll stay clean so you can play them over and over again!

For each game you'll need 1 file folder. Open the folder, and draw the game board on the inside, with squares around the outside of the folder. Choose a corner square as the starting point for the game. Label it "START," then number the rest of the squares around the board in order. Label the last square "FINISH."

Fill in most of the squares with different math problems. Figure out the answers to each problem, and put each on a separate index card so players can check their answers as they play. Make the rest of the squares penalty squares. During the game, anyone landing on a penalty square will have to go back a few spaces or start over, for example. (You get to make up the rules!) Decorate the board by drawing colorful pictures or designs with markers, then cover the board with the clear adhesive paper.

Use small toys or coins for game pieces. Once you've developed all the rules and the object of the game (for example, to be the first to get all the way around the board), play the game with a friend by rolling a die to determine how many squares each player will advance. You can create many different board games—1 for addition problems, 1 for subtraction, 1 for multiplication, etc.

CHALDEAN BOARD GAME

Archaeologists found game boards, which were made more than 4,000 years ago, in the ancient city-state of Ur. Now you can make a game board similar to one the ancient Chaldeans did!

WHAT YOU'LL NEED

3 boxes (cereal boxes work well, but make sure 1 box is much smaller and the other 2 are the same size)
Glue
Paint
Paintbrush
Marker
Bottle caps

Lay the boxes flat, with the smaller box in the middle connecting the other 2 boxes like a bridge. Glue the boxes together, and paint them however you'd like. When the paint is dry, divide the boxes into squares with a marker or paint (the bridge should be only 1 square wide). Paint designs in the squares if you'd like.

Decorate bottle caps for game pieces. Be sure to make 2 sets of game pieces. Make up rules for your game. For example, see who can hop his or her game pieces to the other end and back again (like checkers). Try to line up your markers to block the bridge so your opponent can't get his markers across.

You're the rule maker—make your game as hard or as easy as you'd like!

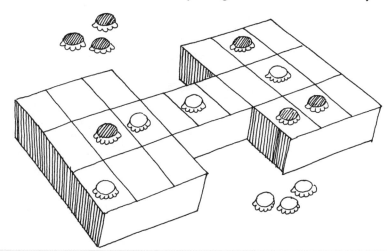

Magic Numbers

Math may have been a very popular subject for ancient Chaldeans. That's because they believed that numbers had special powers that could unlock all the secrets of the universe!

EVERY PENNY COUNTS!

Find out when most pennies in circulation were minted by taking a sampling and graphing the results.

WHAT YOU'LL NEED

100 pennies
Poster board
Markers
Ruler
Craft glue (optional)

This project is most fun when you make a graph with 100 pennies and a friend makes his or her own graph with another 100.

Sort pennies into piles according to the years they were minted. When you have sorted all your pennies, draw a bar graph on poster board, starting with the first year through the most recent. Then chart how many pennies were minted during each of those years. If you don't want to draw a bar graph, you can glue the pennies directly onto poster board to create a graph. (Just don't forget to remove the pennies from the board and clean them after a few days!)

Remember to wash your hands after counting and sorting all the pennies, because coins and bills are very dirty—think of all the hands they've passed through and places they've been!

Backward and Upside Down

Have you have wondered why the picture on the tails side of a coin is always upside down when you flip it from the heads side? Many people have tried to research how this practice started, but no one knows for sure. The United States Mint still follows the tradition of producing all coins with an upside down "coin turn."

EXPRESS YOURSELF

You're an interesting, fun, wonderful person. Let others know all about you! Explore your creativity, your ideas about the world, your own life, and your relationships. Make gifts, write letters, explore your neighborhood, and more. By expressing yourself, you'll not only learn more about you, but you'll also learn more about the world around you.

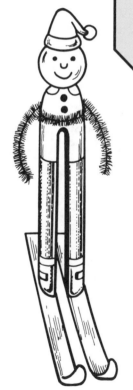

CHALK IT UP

Blending swirls has never been more fun!

WHAT YOU'LL NEED

Colorful chalk
Plain paper or sidewalk (if the weather is warm and dry)
Paper towels

Everyone knows how much fun chalk can be when it comes to games of hopscotch or tic-tac-toe. But have you ever experimented with the swirling strokes of a piece of chalk and discovered what blending can do to those same strokes?

Put 5 thick lines of colored chalk, about 3 inches long, on a paper or sidewalk surface. Make your colorful lines bold and dark, with less than 1 inch between each line. Once your lines are clearly in place, set your chalk down, and get ready to use your fingers.

Start rubbing the first chalk line, blending it toward the thick line of color next to it. Wipe your finger on a paper towel, and repeat the same experiment with the second line of color, letting the lines overlap. Wipe your fingers, and do the same with each line.

What happens as the colors mix? Do the shapes and textures of your lines change? Do shadows and highlights appear? This chalky fun will help teach you how to use color blending to make artistic magic.

Make sure you wear old clothes when you play with chalk. And be sure all the chalk dust is off your clothes, shoes, and hands before you go back into the house.

FRAMED ART

This project gives your artwork a finishing touch.

WHAT YOU'LL NEED

Precut colored mat (available at art supply stores)
Assorted dry pasta
Glitter and sequins (optional)
Craft glue
Magnetic strips
Scissors
Tape

Now your frame can be as attractive as your drawings!

Decorate the mat with assorted shapes of pasta and glitter and sequins. Glue them on the frame in any design you'd like—your design could be random or symmetrical. Let the glue dry. Cut 4 pieces of magnetic strips, and glue them to the back of the mat. Tape your picture to the back of the frame so it shows through the front opening. Use this decorated mat to display your drawings on the refrigerator. Change your picture as often as you like.

TRIP TREASURES

Box up all your holiday keepsakes.

WHAT YOU'LL NEED

Shoe box
Map of your travel route
Glue
Highlighter
Yarn

If you're planning the adventure of a lifetime, why not put together this special treasure box for the things you collect along the way? Wrap the lid and bottom of an ordinary shoe box in an extra highway map of the state you're planning to visit. If possible, wrap the lid of the box so your final destination is easy to see (mark it with a bright colored highlighter). Use a piece of yarn to tie the box securely so you won't lose the special postcards, mementos, and souvenirs of your trip.

CARTOON EVOLUTION

What happens when you mix Superman and Bugs Bunny?

WHAT YOU'LL NEED

Newspapers
Comic strips
Magazines
Old picture books
Scissors
Glue
White paper
Pencil

Everyone loves cartoon characters. There's just something about them that makes us laugh or smile or smirk. But what happens when you mix an old favorite with a new friend? Fun, that's what! And this craft adventure will show you how.

Go through newspapers, comics, magazines, and picture books, and cut out every picture of a cartoon character you find. Set them all out on a table, just to see exactly what you've found. Glue your favorite to a sheet of paper. Then see what kind of updates you can make. Is Mickey Mouse on the page? Why not give him Spider-Man's pants? Add a little feline fluff by tacking on Garfield's tail. Is Mickey hungry? Maybe he'd like a taste of Popeye's spinach. Get creative. Then write a story about your new friend.

Early Animation

Cartoons have been around for longer than most people know. In 1928, Walt Disney created the first animated cartoon featuring Mickey Mouse, *Steamboat Willie*. Do you know what famous full-length animated cartoon was created just a few years later? If you guessed *Snow White and the Seven Dwarfs,* you're right!

ALL THAT GLITTERS

Reflections of light turn your glitter art into sparkling masterpieces.

WHAT YOU'LL NEED

Newspaper
Stiff paper or card stock
Scissors
Hole punch
White glue
Glitter
Waxed paper
String

What is glitter? Most glitter is made up of hundreds and hundreds of tiny metallic plastic bits. Glitter is often made of the same material as those sparkling mylar balloons you see at birthday parties and grand openings. The material's reflective quality catches the light in a dazzling way. This ability to reflect light will turn your glitter art into dazzling masterpieces.

Cover your work surface with newspaper. Cut your favorite shapes out of stiff paper or card stock. Punch a hole in the top of each shape, and cover one side of the shapes with a fine layer of glue. Sprinkle your favorite color of glitter over the shapes. Place the glittered shapes on waxed paper.

As soon as the glue dries, shake the loose glitter onto a sheet of paper. Put the excess glitter back into the bottle to recycle it. Flip the shapes over, and repeat the process for the other sides of the shapes.

Once the glue is dry, thread string through the holes to hang your glittering objects in the sunniest window. You'll soon discover all that glitters is not gold—but it can be pretty stunning. (Be careful not to get bits of glitter in your eyes. Be sure to wash your hands as soon as you have finished this activity.)

TOOTHPICK ARCHITECTURE

Create a tiny city, geometric shapes, or a circus tent with clowns.
You can build whatever your imagination dreams up.

EASY

WHAT YOU'LL NEED

Waxed paper
Plastic-based clay
Flat, round, or
    colored tooth-
    picks
Poster board

Place a sheet of waxed paper over your work surface. Roll the plastic-based clay into several ¼- to ½-inch balls. The number of balls you need to make will depend on what you're making, since the clay balls are the anchor joints of your toothpick creation. To make a person, you will need 7 balls of clay; to make a pyramid shape, you will need 4 balls of clay.

Insert a toothpick into a ball of clay. Connect the toothpicks with the clay balls until you have completed your structure. Place your finished projects on a piece of poster board to display your handiwork.

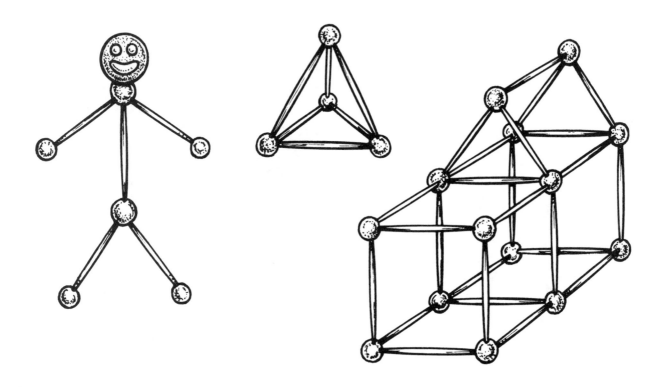

PAPER ROSES

Watch these tissue flowers bloom before your eyes.

WHAT YOU'LL NEED

Tissues
Floral wire
Scissors
Floral tape (optional)
Floral perfume
   (optional)

People love getting flowers, but they hate seeing the delicate petals fade and fall. These lovely tissue paper flowers never wilt, and they're easy to make.

Take a single tissue (the kind you wipe your nose with), and spread it out flat in front of you. The long sides of the tissue should be on the top and bottom, the short sides on the right and left. Fold about ½ inch of the bottom of the tissue up. Then fan-fold the next ½ inch to the back. Keep fan-folding the tissue until it is all folded.

Once you have the tissue folded into what looks like a long strip, fold it again, this time matching the short ends to each other—it will have a single bend in the center. Take a 12-inch piece of wire, and tightly bind the center of the strip. Cut the folded end. Begin to peel the layers of tissue, opening the flower to form a fluffy, round blossom.

Wrap the very bottom of the flower (where the wire holds the tissue) and the wire with floral tape. Very lightly mist the flower with perfume. Enjoy your flower—it will last a long, long time if you're careful with it.

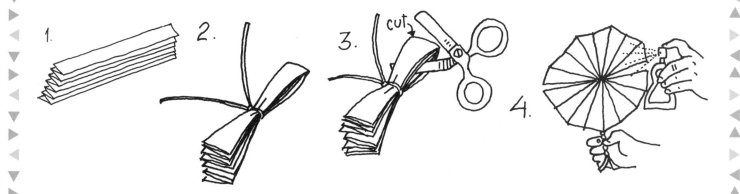

BABY BOX PUZZLE

This cut-up fun will puzzle you silly.

MEDIUM⁺

Adult Help Needed

WHAT YOU'LL NEED

9 small gelatin or
   pudding boxes
Ruler
Scissors
Drawing paper
Crayons or markers
White glue
Craft knife (adult
   use only)

Ever wanted to make your own puzzle? Check out this 9-piece adventure. Gather the 9 gelatin or pudding boxes together, and place the boxes in a square with 3 across and 3 down. Measure this square, and then measure and cut a piece of drawing paper to this size. Draw a picture on the paper—make it anything you want. It might be your favorite cartoon character, your favorite rock star, even a picture of yourself. When you are finished with your picture, place it face down on the table. Cover the back of your picture with a thick layer of glue.

Put a box, widest side down, in the upper left-hand corner of the picture. Lay the next box flush against the end of the first. Lay the third box against the end of the second. Make a second row of boxes, then a third. Be sure the boxes are set as close together as possible. Once the glue has completely dried and hardened, have a parent use a craft knife to cut the boxes apart. (Only adults should use a craft knife!) You'll wind up with a 9-piece puzzle, custom-made with your favorite subject in mind.

For even more fun, add another picture to the back of the boxes for a 2-sided puzzle!

SPIN ART

This art project will have your head spinning. Watch as paints mix and swirl to become new colors.

MEDIUM

Adult Help Needed

WHAT YOU'LL NEED

Cardboard box (with high sides)
Nail
Cork or small wood block and hammer
Newspaper
Scissors
Drawing paper or construction paper
Removable tape
Poster paints
Water

With an adult's help, carefully push a nail down through the middle of the bottom of a cardboard box so the nail pokes through to the outside of the box. Push a cork onto the nail, or use a hammer to gently tap a wood block onto the nail. (We've shortened the sides of the box in the illustration so you can better see how to construct your spin box. Your box should have high sides to prevent paint from splattering.)

Cover your work area with newspaper. Cut a piece of paper to fit inside the box. Tape the paper to the sides of the box to hold it in place. Put dabs of slightly watered-down poster paint on the paper. Hold the cork (or wood block), and spin the box. The paint will fly toward the sides of the box. Untape the paper from the box. Place your artwork on newspaper to dry.

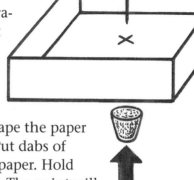

Too Soon to Fly?

Leonardo da Vinci is best remembered as the painter of the Mona Lisa, in the early 1500s. But he's almost equally famous for his other astonishing talents, including architecture, sculpture, and engineering. In fact, in his spare time he drew parachutes and flying machines that actually resembled inventions of the 19th and 20th centuries!

MASK OF MAGIC

This mysterious mask will help your imagination soar.

WHAT YOU'LL NEED

White cardboard or card stock
Pencil
Scissors
Craft glue
Sequins, colored paper, glitter glue, ribbons, feathers, and other craft supplies
Elastic, string, or yarn
Stapler and staples

Masked balls were all the rage in centuries past. Kings and dukes, queens and fair ladies wore lovely masks to hide their identities until the ball came to a close. You can make your own mysterious mask.

Use the small mask design on this page as a pattern—or design your own shape! Draw your mask on the cardboard or card stock. Carefully cut out holes for your eyes. Decorate your mask with things you find around the house. Add sparkling sequins or bits of bright paper. Use glitter glue to add sparkle. Add dangling ribbons to the bottom or feathers to the top. (Be careful not to get sequins in your eyes. Don't use glitter on your mask; it could get in your eyes.)

Express yourself in your mask, no matter how wild or outrageous it may seem. Once your design is complete, staple a piece of elastic or 2 pieces of string or yarn to either side of the mask. Place the mask on your face, and the mystery of your identity is safe. The magic is sure to begin!

CLOTHESPIN BUTTERFLY

Pin down a fluttering friend.

WHAT YOU'LL NEED

White paper
Pencil
Ruler
Scissors
Colored paper
Sequins
Craft glue
Clothespin
Wiggle eyes
Chenille stems
Magnetic strip
(optional)

Butterflies are amazing things. They flutter in the wind like real-life fairies, colorfully floating on air. You can make your own butterflies with paper, glue, and clothespins—and a little imagination.

Draw a 5×5-inch bow-tie shape on a piece of white paper, making sure the shape narrows to about 1 inch at the center. Cut out the shape; this is your butterfly. Decorate the wings with bits of paper, sequins—anything colorful. Glue the butterfly to the bottom of a clothespin. Add wiggle eyes and chenille-stem antennae to your butterfly.

Now you've got a magical butterfly you need never set free! Add a magnetic strip to the bottom of the clothespin, and your butterfly becomes a refrigerator magnet. It can hold notes, your report card, and coupons for mom!

COFFEE CAN BUG

Make some plastic insects you can keep or catch.

WHAT YOU'LL NEED
Coffee can lid
Construction paper
Pencil
Scissors
Craft glue
Markers
Chenille stems
(optional)

Grown-ups may use coffee as a morning eye opener, but these fun, flying coffee can bugs are even better reasons for them to drink up!

Take the plastic freshness lid from an empty coffee can (ask for permission before you take it). Decide what type of bug you'd like to make, and choose construction paper colors that correspond to that bug—if you were making a ladybug you would use red paper. Trace a circle on a piece of construction paper using the lid. Cut out the circle just inside the line so it is a little smaller than the lid. Glue the paper to the top of the plastic lid.

Decorate your bug, maybe adding a black head and black spots for a ladybug, green wings and big eyes for a fly, or purple and pink for a bug from your imagination! If you'd like, add chenille stems for antennae.

Now it's time to toss your colorful insect through the air and see how it flies. For extra fun, set up bowls or boxes as targets and assign them points. Have a contest with a friend to see whose bug can accumulate the most points.

CLOTHESPIN PEOPLE

Create your own action figures—family members, super heroes, or even an Olympic ski team!

You don't have to spend all your hard-earned allowance money on toys—make your dolls or action figures yourself!

Cover your work surface with newspaper. Paint clothes on your clothespin person, letting each color of paint dry before you paint on another color. Paint shoes on the bottom ½ inch of clothespin. Paint pants on the slotted "legs." Paint the shirt on the top part of the clothespin body. (Leave the knob unpainted.)

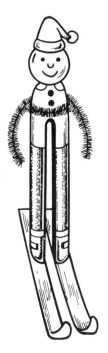

Draw a face on the knob of the clothespin using fine-point markers. To make the arms, wrap a chenille stem around the middle of the shirt and glue it in place. Cut a hat from felt, and glue it on top of the head. To make a skier, cut small paper skis out of construction paper and glue them to the bottoms of the clothespin legs.

Now create other clothespin guys and gals! How about a parachuting clothespin skydiver?!

Beautiful Finish

In Japan, the very oldest examples of traditional handmade Japanese dolls were carved from wood. Instead of painting the wood, the doll makers used a heavy finish made of ground sea shells, called "gofun." The gofun finish is so beautiful that seldom are details painted over it.

CRAFTY ANIMALS

These soft and cuddly animals will never run away from home.

WHAT YOU'LL NEED

Cardboard
Scissors
Craft glue
Yarn
Paper scraps

It's hard to believe you can turn cardboard and scrap yarn into fun animals, but it's true!

Cut 3 strips of scrap cardboard; make 2 the same length and the other about 2 inches longer. The longest strip will be the body, neck, and head of the animal. The other strips will be the animal's legs. Make a bend in the longer piece of cardboard, about ¼ of the way down from an end; make another bend another ¼ of the way down from the first bend. This is the head and neck of the animal. Your animal should look a bit like a backward Z.

Bend the shorter 2 pieces in half. Fold 1 over the "shoulders" of the animal, just behind the neck, and the other at the opposite end or "bottom" of the animal. (You'll need to rebend the legs so they lay flat on top of the animal's body.) Glue the legs in place.

Wrap your animal's body with yarn. Work your way down the body, circling it again and again with soft, fluffy yarn, passing over the legs at first. Once the body is covered, slowly work your way back to the legs and start wrapping those pieces of cardboard until they are covered and plump. Work your way back up to the belly of the animal, and tie off the loose end of yarn. Glue on scraps of yarn for ears, a mane, and a tail. Use bits of paper to add animal eyes and other features.

Make a zoo full of animals!

A VISUAL "DIARY"

You'll remember your next nature trip long after it's over
when you create this "natural wonders" wall hanging.

DIFFICULT

WHAT YOU'LL NEED
Small nature objects
4 sticks or twigs
Jute twine
Craft glue
Wire or small hooks

When you go on a nature hike, collect small objects such as twigs, grasses, flowers, nuts, bark, and shells. When you get home, you can weave all the objects together to make an artistic record of your trip!

First, make a frame for your artwork. Lay the 4 sticks or twigs so they form a square or rectangle. Tie the corners together with the jute twine. You are now going to make a grid on the frame. Wrap the jute twine around the frame from top to bottom and then from side to side, creating a grid. Each row should be about ¼ inch away from the next row when you wind the twine.

Use this twine base to mount the nature objects on. You can weave them through the twine, use small hooks or pieces of wire to hook them on, or glue them on. You can attach the objects to the frame in the order you found them or in an artistic design.

After all that crafting, you'll have a unique "diary" of your trip.

A Historical Document
Diaries are fascinating because they portray everyday lives in a given time and place. One of the most famous diaries belonged to Mary Chestnut, who wrote about her life during the American Civil War. What would your diary tell people in the future about events making history today?

HAIR-CLIP HOLDER

Keep your hair—and your room—a little neater with this friendly face.

WHAT YOU'LL NEED

Stiff cardboard
Scissors
Markers
Yarn
Craft glue

If you're always losing your hair clips and scrunchies, you need someplace to keep them. This fun project is a great idea for organizing your "hair things."

Cut a 4-inch circle from stiff cardboard. This is your hair-clip holder's "face." Draw on eyes, lips, freckles, dimples—anything that makes you smile.

Cut sixteen 20-inch pieces of colored yarn to make your hair-clip holder's "hair." Tie the yarn pieces in the middle with a small piece of matching yarn to form the "part." Glue the part to the top of your cardboard face. You can either braid the dangling strands of yarn hair or leave them loose.

Now you can keep all your hair ties and barrettes safely clipped in your holder's hair until you're ready to use them!

SWITCHPLATE COVERS

Switch on some fun with this stylish room accent!

EASY

Adult Help Needed

WHAT YOU'LL NEED

Plastic juice or bleach bottle (washed and rinsed well)
Scissors
Pencil
Paints
Paintbrushes
Craft supplies (sequins, rhinestones, markers, etc.)
Craft glue
Double-sided tape

Tired of seeing that dull old switchplate every time you flip your lights on and off? Why not make a new design that shines with your own ideas?

Cut a piece of plastic from a clean, washed bleach or juice bottle. Ask an adult to unscrew the faceplate in your room so you can use it as a pattern. Place the faceplate on the plastic, trace around it, and cut out the rectangle. (Have an adult replace the faceplate.) Mark and cut out the center rectangle to make room for the switch.

Decorate the plastic any way that suits your mood. Add sequins or rhinestones if you're in a glamorous mood. Draw tiger stripes if you're feeling wild. Doodle hearts and flowers if you're feeling full of love. Or make it galactic with stars and asteroids if you're an out-of-this-world kid.

When you're done decorating it, attach your new, improved switchplate over the old one (the old switchplate must be in place to keep you safe from electricity) with double-sided tape.

Quiet Genius

If it wasn't for Thomas Edison, you might still be lighting your room with a candle, wondering when someone would invent better lighting. But did you know that when Edison invented the first practical electrical lightbulb, in 1879, he was almost completely deaf?

HARDWARE SCULPTURE

Nail down a fun metal sculpture.

MEDIUM

Adult Help Needed

**WHAT YOU'LL
NEED**
Hardware (washers,
nails, nuts,
screws, bolts,
etc.)
Household cement

As hard as it is to believe, you can make a great sculpture with nothing more than nuts, bolts, screws, and other hardware. This fun and unusual activity will show you how.

Ask your parents to go through their spare hardware, or head for a hardware store to get started. Pick out a good-size washer, some tiny nails, drapery hooks, and anything else that captures your imagination. Have an adult help you glue the hardware together using household cement. (Be sure the room is well ventilated, and keep the glue out of your eyes.)

Want to make a ladybug? Try a washer with 6 tiny nail legs and miniature nut eyes. A spider? Have an adult help you bend 8 long nails and attach them to a washer, with a rounded nut for the spider's silvery head. You are only limited by your supplies and your imagination. Hitting the nail on the head has never been more fun!

Buttery Sculpture

To celebrate the New Year, Buddhist monks in Tibet create elaborate yak-butter sculptures to illustrate a different story or fable each year. The sculptures can reach 30 feet high, and they are lit with special butter lamps. Awards are given for the best butter sculptures!

DRESSY HANKY

Paint one of your Grandma's or Grandpa's favorite things on this special hanky.

EASY

Adult Help Needed

WHAT YOU'LL NEED
White handkerchief
Wax crayons
Damp towels
Iron

To make a dressy hanky, draw a design on a plain white handkerchief with a wax crayon. Press firmly so the wax really sticks to the fabric. Think of a design your grandma or grandpa would really like. Do they have a favorite color? A favorite pet or flower? Draw something that will let them know you are thinking about them. You might want to sign your name, and add a message. When you are satisfied with your design, put the handkerchief between 2 damp towels and ask an adult to help you press it with a warm iron. The wax will melt, and most of the dye from the crayons will stay in the cloth for a permanent design. A handmade hanky is a thoughtful and personal gift. It's useful, too!

TOOTHPICK TOWER

Stacking toothpicks is harder than you think.

MEDIUM⁺

WHAT YOU'LL NEED
Clean, large bottle
Toothpicks

Sliding 1 toothpick across the mouth of a bottle is easy. But stacking 10 or 20 toothpicks across the same small space is a challenge you'll have fun attempting, with or without a play partner.

Clean the bottle well with soap and water. Take 10 toothpicks in your hand. Start stacking them across the mouth of the bottle, then stack them across the first layer you set down. See how many toothpicks you can safely stack without knocking the whole experiment down. Store your toothpick game pieces inside your bottle after you're done playing.

HAMMER A LION

Pound out a wild work of art using this guide.

DIFFICULT

WHAT YOU'LL NEED
Paper
Pencil
Wood block
Small nails
Hammer

If you like lions, you'll love the chance to create one . . . using a block of wood and ordinary nails!

Draw a lion on a piece of paper. Imprint the design into your block of wood by placing the picture on the wood. Then retrace the lines with a pencil, pressing extra hard.

Now that you have the outline of the lion in the wood, hammer nails into the block of wood along the lines. Before you know it, you'll have 3-dimensional art you can keep or give proudly as a gift.

Remember this activity isn't limited to a lion—you can create your own special design. Do you have a friend who just loves koalas? How about Aunt Jane who collects elephants? And don't limit yourself to just animals—there are lots of objects that would make great pictures!

MARBLE MENAGERIE

Round out your animal collection with this marble magic.

MEDIUM

WHAT YOU'LL NEED
Stiff cardboard
Ruler
Scissors
Markers
Colored marbles
Craft glue
Colored paper

If you love marbles and animals, this is the activity for you.

Cut a small piece of stiff cardboard about 4×6 inches long. Decorate it so it looks like an animal habitat or a cuddly pet bed. Now, follow the patterns at the bottom of this page to make a marble mate—or try some creatures of your own! Make a turtle (a circle of marbles for the shell, 1 marble each for the turtle's head, feet, and stubby tail), snake (6 marbles laid end to end), or a marble cat (a pyramid of marbles with paper ears and tail added).

Cut out small pieces of paper for eyes, ears, and other body parts to finish your creatures; add the details to the paper with markers. When the glue is dry, put your animal in its habitat!

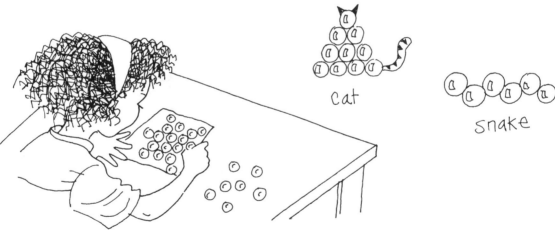

cat

snake

Presidential Marbles

If you enjoy playing marbles, then you have something in common with several past presidents of the United States. It's said that George Washington and Thomas Jefferson both enjoyed the game of marbles and Abraham Lincoln was an expert at a marble game called "old bowler."

PAPER MAGIC BEADS

Paper makes gorgeous beads!

DIFFICULT

WHAT YOU'LL
🪙🪙 **NEED** 🪙🪙
Decorative paper
Ruler
Pencil
Scissors
Clear gel glue
Water
Teaspoon
Small margarine tub
Plastic straws
Embroidery floss

Think used paper is just for recycling? Not anymore! Now you can make great jewelry with it! Use whatever decorative paper you want, which can include gift wrap or the Sunday comics. On the backside of the paper, use the ruler and pencil to draw triangles that are 1 inch across the bottom and 7 inches tall. Make as many triangles as you want beads, then cut out the triangles.

Mix 2 teaspoons of clear gel glue with 1 teaspoon of water in the small margarine tub. Dip a triangle in the glue mixture, and let the excess glue drip off. Wrap the triangle around the straw, pattern side up, starting with the wide end. Wrap all the triangles in the same way, and let them dry for a day. Remove the straw.

Now it's time to string your Paper Magic Beads to make a necklace, bracelet, anklet, or any other piece of jewelry you'd like to make!

CLAY 'N' CANDLES

A little heart can house the glow.

EASY

WHAT YOU'LL
🪙🪙 **NEED** 🪙🪙
Air-drying clay
6-inch candle
Paint
Paintbrush
Glitter
Sequins

For a candleholder that expresses warmth and love, check out this fun project. Form a 3-inch ball of clay into a special shape you admire—it could be a circle, a triangle, a heart, or anything else that catches your fancy. Press the base of the candle into the center of the clay shape. Paint the shape if you'd like. Press in glitter and sequins on the surface of the shape, and let the clay dry. Before you know it, you'll have a lovely, handmade candleholder to brighten up your day (and night). (Remember, never light a candle without adult supervision!)

SCRATCH BOARD

Etch a design on scratch board, and you'll see the contrast between dramatic black and bold brights.

Cover your work surface with newspaper. Color a piece of card stock or poster board with crayons in assorted colors, covering the paper completely with a thick layer—color very hard. Mix black poster paint and 2 drops of dish soap together. Paint the mixture over the layer of crayon coloring. Let the paint mixture dry completely. Use a nail file to scratch off the paint in a design or a picture, just as if you were drawing a picture on a piece of paper. Now your picture practically jumps off the paper!

IN A NUTSHELL

Tiny animal habitats come to life on the half shell.

These tiny animals in nutty habitats are cute and never need to be fed. Cover the inside of half a walnut shell with glue. Sprinkle a thin layer of hobby store grass (it's like green sawdust) inside the nut. Add a tiny paper bush or watering hole, and then glue a small plastic animal in this cozy, fun place. Once the glue is dry, you'll have the world's teeniest pet zone. Take this a pocket-size pal everywhere you go, or you can give it as a gift!

BIB PUPPETS

Try on a whole new look—stand behind the bib.

WHAT YOU'LL  NEED

Butcher paper
Pencil
Scissors
Paints
Paintbrush
String
Camera or video-
    tape recorder

Most of us have seen those fun wooden screens at amusement parks and tourist spots where you slip your head through a hole and appear as if you've become a cowboy or a dinosaur. Create your own crazy optical illusions by making body-size bib puppet outfits you can stand behind.

Draw a headless animal or space alien outfit on a large piece of butcher paper. Craft it as crazy as you like—create something that will make everyone laugh. Cut out your creation, and paint it. When the paint is dry, have an adult help you suspend the bib puppet with pieces of string so you can peek your head over the top.

Have your friends or parents take your picture or videotape you. You'll get a whole new perspective on who you are and what you look like. For more fun, turn the pictures into postcards to send to your grandparents or someone who would enjoy hearing from you—and seeing you!

WORD CHAIN

Explore and express how you feel, one word at a time.

**WHAT YOU'LL
NEED**

Paper
Crayons, markers,
or colored
pencils

Sometimes the reasons for our moods hide at the back of our minds. We might be really happy or just a little sad and not quite understand why we feel what we feel. If you ever wonder what you're feeling and why, try this fun word game to help you find out.

Pick a word that seems to describe what you are feeling. It might be "excited" or "blue," it might be "confused" or "angry." Pick whatever word best describes how you think you feel. Write it out in a color that matches the mood.

Now, ask yourself why you feel that way: parents, puppy, best friend, weather. Write the first word that comes to your mind in a color that helps describe it. But here's the trick. Try to build that word on the word you already wrote, like a crossword puzzle. Keep up with the game until the page is full or you run out of words.

Doing this game may help you understand yourself a little better!

SNOWSTORM ART

You don't need snow to create a snowstorm. Starch or glue and a little rice will make a dazzling storm!

WHAT YOU'LL NEED

Dark construction paper (black is best)
Markers or crayons
Liquid starch or glue
Paintbrush or cotton swabs
Uncooked rice

Love the winter weather, even when it's too cold outside to play? Well, make a winter project in your warm house that expresses how much you love the snow!

Draw a winter scene on the construction paper. Do you like sledding or building snow creatures? Then draw that! A pretty cabin in the woods with smoke curling out of the chimney would also make a pretty picture. Create whatever scene you'd like.

When you are done drawing and coloring your picture, brush a generous amount of starch or glue over your picture on the construction paper. Sprinkle the rice over the glue on the paper. Shake off the excess rice and discard. (Don't put the rice back in the package—you won't want to be eating starched or glued rice for dinner!)

Now watch out for the blizzard!

AWESOME AQUARIUM

This aquarium doesn't contain real fish, but people will give it a second glance because it looks so awesome!

WHAT YOU'LL NEED

Construction paper
Pencil
Scissors
Sandwich-size seal-
    able bag
Markers or crayons
Stapler and staples
Colorful gravel
Easter grass
Glue

Draw and cut out a fish-bowl shape from construction paper—make sure the shape is smaller than the size of the sandwich bags you have. Place the fish-bowl shape in the center of a different color of construction paper, and trace the shape. Cut out the paper inside the drawn lines (this will be called paper #1). You want the shape you cut out to be a bit smaller than the fish bowl shape you traced. Do the same to a second sheet of construction paper (this will be called paper #2).

Draw a few fish on construction paper. Decorate them however you'd like—you can be realistic, or you can be whimsical! Cut out the fish shapes.

Using paper #1, staple the plastic bag around the edge of the cutout on all sides except the top. Put a handful of gravel in the bag, some Easter grass arranged like seaweed, and the paper fish you've drawn and cut out. Arrange the fish any way you want—glue them in place inside the bag.

Seal the bag, and staple the top to the paper. The bag should be stapled all the way around the edge of the cutout. Glue paper #2 over the top of paper #1, covering up the staples. To finish, glue the fish-bowl shape to the back of paper #1.

AROUND THE WORLD

The world is a big, exciting place, full of amazing people from many different nations who have many interesting customs. You don't need to be a world traveler to explore all those nations and customs—all you need is a curious mind and some fun projects from this book. You'll make games, baskets, lanterns, shoes, and much more. It's time to begin your adventures!

PORTABLE SOCCER GAME

Baseball and football aren't the most popular sports in the world—soccer is! Now you can enjoy this game no matter where you live with this portable, tabletop version.

WHAT YOU'LL NEED

Berry basket
Scissors
Large rectangular piece of cardboard
Twist ties
Green and white paint or markers
Paintbrush (optional)
Aluminum foil

Cut the berry basket in half; each half will be a goal. Place a berry-basket goal in the middle of the short end of the cardboard. Start on the right side of the berry basket. Poke 2 holes next to each other in the cardboard—1 on the inside of the basket, the other on the outside. Repeat for the left side of the basket. Attach the goal to the cardboard by bending a twist tie through each pair of holes in the cardboard. Twist the tie ends together underneath the cardboard. Repeat the process for the other short side of the cardboard with the other berry-basket goal.

Paint or use markers to make the cardboard look like a soccer field, using green for grass and white for the boundary lines. Make a ball from foil. Turn your hand into a soccer player—use your pointer and middle fingers as legs to kick the ball.

It's now time to find an opponent and start playing!

TURQUOISE BRACELETS

Design jewelry that looks like turquoise pieces worn by
Native Americans in the West.

MEDIUM

Adult Help Needed

WHAT YOU'LL NEED

Paper towel tube
Ruler
Scissors
Aluminum foil
Rubbing alcohol
Measuring cup
Small glass bowl
Blue and green food
    coloring
Macaroni shells
Spoon
Paper towels
Craft glue

Cut a paper towel tube into 1½-inch-wide bands.
Check to see if the tube will slide onto your wrist. If it
doesn't, cut the tube so it forms a C. Cover the bracelet
with aluminum foil.

Put ½ cup rubbing alcohol in a small glass bowl. Add a
few drops of blue food coloring and 1 drop of green food
coloring. Stir the colors to blend them. Color the macaroni
shells by placing a few at a time into the glass bowl.
Remove the macaroni from the alcohol mixture with a
spoon, and place them on a paper towel to dry. Continue
until all the macaroni shells are colored. An adult should
dispose of the rubbing alcohol when done.

When the macaroni shells are dry, glue them to
the covered bands to make bracelets. All your friends
will want some of your stunning "turquoise and silver" jewelry!

A Lucky Stone

Native American Indians in the West consider turquoise to be the stone of
happiness, health, and good fortune. In addition to using turquoise to make
beautiful jewelry, some nations keep good luck objects in bowls
painted with crushed turquoise.

HUICHOL INDIAN YARN PICTURE

Tell a story with a yarn picture, as the Huichol Indians
of western Mexico do.

WHAT YOU'LL NEED

Pencil
Cardboard
Scissors
Yarn
Glue
Craft stick

Brilliant Huichol pictures depict stories about the Indians' myths, religion, and history. To make your own colorful yarn picture, draw an outline of an animal, person, plant, or object on a piece of cardboard. Then cut and glue pieces of yarn on the outline to cover it— use the craft stick to apply the glue to the cardboard. If you'd like, continue to add additional strands of yarn inside the outline, "painting" with yarn, until the design is filled with color. Place yarn pieces close together so that only the yarn, and not the cardboard, shows. After the picture has been filled, you can use another color of yarn to fill up the space outside the animal, person, plant, or object your story is about.

DANCE THE RAIN DOWN

Make a rainmaker shaker, and, in the tradition of many
Native American and African peoples, dance and play music
to invite the skies to rain!

WHAT YOU'LL NEED

Cardboard tube
Stapler
Beans, buttons, or
   other small
   objects
Paint
Paintbrush

When doing their rain dances, rainmakers in Uganda shake handmade rattles that sound like rain. To make a rainmaker shaker, staple 1 end of a cardboard tube closed. Fill the tube with beans, buttons, or other small objects that will make noise. Then staple the other end to seal the rattle. Paint the tube, and let it dry. When it's dry outside, invent a dance using the rainmaker and invite the sky to bring forth water!

RAKHI (HINDU PLAITED BRACELET)

These plaited bracelets are given to family members at Raksha Bandhan, a festival celebrated by most Hindu and Sikh families. You can give your rakhi to a family member or friend, too.

MEDIUM

WHAT YOU'LL 👀 NEED 👀

Strips of fabric, yarn, string, or ribbon

Piece of corkboard or cardboard

Pins

Small circle of cardboard

Aluminum foil

Sequins

Craft glue

Markers

Needle and thread

Use strips of fabric or pieces of string that are more than double the length of the bracelet you want. To make a 3-strand rakhi, knot the ends of 3 pieces of ribbon or fabric together. Pin the ribbon or fabric to a corkboard or piece of heavy cardboard so it is easier to work with.

Braid the ribbons or fabric pieces as shown in the diagram. Continue braiding in this manner until you have braided almost all of the length of ribbon or fabric. To finish the plait, knot the ends of the ribbon or fabric together.

Decorate a small circle of cardboard with foil, sequins, and markers. Sew the decorated circle to the middle of the plaited band. To wear the plait as a bracelet, tie it around your wrist.

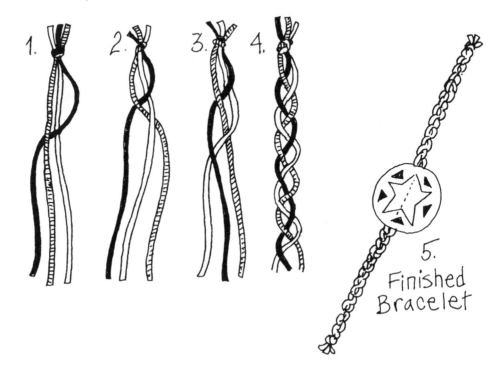

1.   2.   3.   4.

5. Finished Bracelet

STORYBOOK QUILT

Stitch together squares of family pictures, sayings, stories, and more to make a quilt that tells the story of your family.

WHAT YOU'LL NEED

Poster paper
Ruler
Scissors
Family pictures
Markers
Clear vinyl adhesive
    paper
Hole punch
Large plastic needle
Yarn

Cut the poster paper into 6×6-inch squares. Make as many as you'd like, but make enough so that there are the same number down as across when placed as a grid pattern (for example, 4 down and 4 across).

Glue a picture of each family member on a separate square (don't forget your pets). Then write anecdotes, family sayings, or anything else that explains who your family really is. When all the squares are completed, cover each one with clear vinyl adhesive paper.

Use a ruler to measure and punch holes around the outer edges of the squares. Be sure the holes of each square line up with the holes of the squares next to it. Thread a large plastic needle with yarn, and sew the squares together for a Family Storybook Quilt.

Hang your quilt with pride!

SAHARA SAND SHOES

Make these desert sand shoes like ones the Tuaregs, a wandering
desert tribe, made so they could travel on the hot sand
and not burn their feet.

Trace the shape of your foot onto a piece of heavy cardboard. Draw a paddle
shape around the foot pattern—the shape should bulge out at the heel and toes
and come in closer at the sides of your foot. Trace your other foot the same way,
and make another paddle shape around it.

Have an adult help you cut 4 of these cardboard paddle shapes for each foot.
Also cut 4 strips (about 2 inches wide and 4 inches long) from thinner cardboard
for shoe straps. Glue 4 paddle shapes together, 1 on top of the other (using lots
of glue), for each shoe. Glue the ends of the 2 cardboard strips (1 on each side of
the shoe) between the top 2 layers of the paddle shapes. The strips should be
angled toward the toes of the shoes. Put something heavy on top of each shoe
until the glue dries completely.

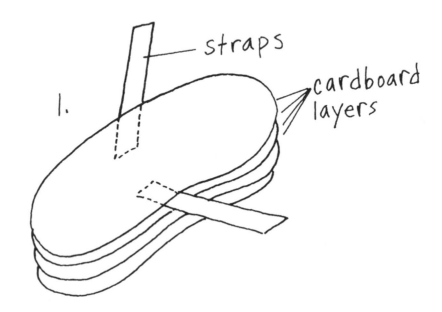

1.

straps

cardboard
layers

Paint designs on the shoes and straps. Place your feet on the shoes. On the top of each sole, make a line between your big toe and second toe. Ask an adult to use a nail to punch 2 holes close together on each line. The holes should go through all the layers of cardboard.

For each shoe and going from the top to the bottom, thread a shoelace through 1 hole, in and out of a button on the bottom, and back through the other hole. Fold the thin cardboard strips inward so they cross over the holes in the sole. Punch 2 holes through the crossed strips. Thread the shoelace through the holes in the strips and through a second button. Try the shoe on. The shoelace goes between your big toe and second toe. Slide the button down until the shoe fits securely on your feet. Tie the shoelace.

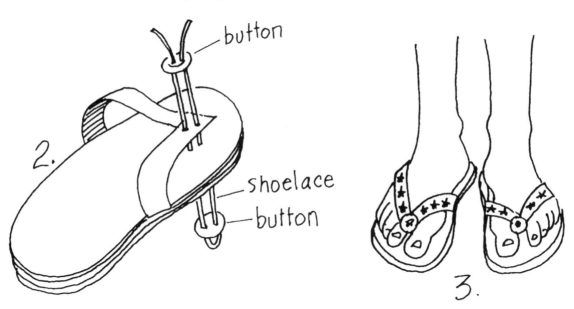

Beautiful Desert Music

The Tuaregs are a nomadic people who wander and live in the Sahara. Their music is beautiful and is often played during their tea time, accompanied by hand claps and a chorus of women. The words to the music tell the stories of their wanderings through deserts, mountains, and villages.

PAPER MOSAIC

Original mosaics were made with small pieces of tiles. You'll use small pieces of paper to make this mosaic. Awesome!

Adult Help Needed

WHAT YOU'LL NEED
Scratch paper
Pencil
White drawing
   paper
Scissors
Construction paper
Colored foil
   (optional)
Wallpaper sample
   pages (optional)
Paper cutter
   (optional)
Glue stick

Make a sketch of a scene on a piece of scratch paper. Fill the entire piece of paper with the scene (flowers, birds, tropical fish, and fruit are things that work well for this). When you are happy with your sketch, draw it again on the drawing paper.

With scissors, make ½-inch strips of the colored paper, foil, and wallpaper samples. If you have a paper cutter, have an adult make the strips. Cut the strips into small squares. Again, an adult can do this on the paper cutter, or you can do it with scissors.

Paste the paper onto the objects in your picture, and use the colors you have creatively. An apple, for example, can have many colors: light red, dark red, and red/brown that could be used to show shading. Place the squares as close together as possible, leaving white paper showing through to look as though the mosaics are embedded in plaster.

When you are done with your picture, mount the finished work on a larger sheet of construction paper for display.

CANADA DAY FLAG

On July 1 (Canada Day), wave a Canadian flag you created using construction paper and paint.

WHAT YOU'LL NEED
Red paint
Paint tray or pie tin
Large maple leaf
White construction paper
Paintbrush
12-inch stick
Tape

Pour some paint into a tray or pie tin, and dip the leaf into the paint to coat 1 side of it thoroughly. Press the leaf in the center of the white paper, and carefully lift the leaf up. Paint the outside ends of the paper to make the Canadian flag (see illustration). When the paint is dry, tape your flag to the stick. Proudly wave the Canadian flag to celebrate Canada Day on July 1!

SILLY SANDWICHES

You can't eat these "sandwiches," but you'll have fun coming up with all sorts of silly ingredients!

WHAT YOU'LL NEED
Construction paper
Scissors
Glue
Markers
Hole punch
Other craft supplies

Cut out 4 light brown or white pieces of construction paper in the shape of a piece of bread. Glue 3 edges of 2 bread-shaped pieces together, leaving an edge unglued. When the glue is dry, stuff small scraps of paper between the 2 layers. Glue the open end closed. Repeat for the other 2 pieces of bread-shaped paper. Then cut out other ingredients to fill your sandwich. Lettuce could be made from green paper, crumpled up, then glued to a bread slice. Tomato slices could be "stuffed" to look more realistic (just as you did with the bread slices). Use markers, the hole punch (to make Swiss cheese), and any other craft supplies you'd like to make your sandwich.

When you're done making all your ingredients, glue the layers together to make delicious-looking artwork!

OJO DE DIOS

Weave yarn around two sticks or twigs to create an ancient Mexican "Eye of God."

MEDIUM

WHAT YOU'LL NEED
2 twigs or craft sticks
Craft glue
Yarn
Scissors

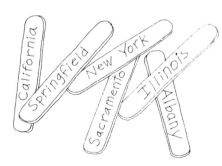

To make your Ojo de Dios, glue 2 craft sticks together to create a cross shape. Or, if you use twigs, cross them and tie them together by winding yarn around the middle diagonally in 1 direction and then diagonally in the other direction.

After you have formed the cross, tie a strand of yarn to the center and begin to weave it around the arms. Weave the yarn over and around 1 arm and then over and around the next arm. Continue in this way around all the arms. Change colors by tying a new piece of yarn to the end of the piece you have been using, and keep winding. Continue until the entire shape is covered, then cut and tuck the end of the yarn into the weaving. Add a dot of glue to hold the end in place.

Hang your Ojo de Dios in your room, or give it as a gift to someone special.

STATE CAPITALS MATCHING GAME

This game, made with craft sticks, really comes in handy when you want to know your states and capitals.

MEDIUM

WHAT YOU'LL NEED
Reference books
100 large craft sticks
Markers

Print the names of all the states on craft sticks. Next, print the name of each state capital on a separate stick. On the back of matching sticks, you can draw the state flower or state bird for each set. Then when you play the game, you'll know that if the backs match, you've correctly matched the state with its capital. Now it's time to play the game! Lay all the sticks on a big table or on the floor. See if you can match the states to their capitals.

TIME CAPSULE

Time capsules help people in the future understand past cultures. Help future generations learn about your life!

Easy

Adult Help Needed

WHAT YOU'LL NEED

Various objects
Paper
Pen
Resealable plastic container
Plastic bag
Shovel

Gather objects that represent the current year. These can be baseball cards, newspapers, magazines, fashion items, or anything else you can imagine. You might write a letter that tells about you, your family, or your community. Put these items into a plastic container, and seal it securely. Put the plastic container into a plastic bag, and tie the bag closed.

Find someplace to bury the time capsule; make sure you have permission to do so. Dig a 3-foot hole in the ground, put your time capsule in, and cover it with dirt. Make a sign and put it on the ground above the capsule, or make a map to the capsule. On your map or sign, indicate what year the time capsule should be opened. When it is opened, people will find artifacts that will give them some information about how you lived.

SEED KEEPING

Many people save seeds from their gardens so they can be used to start next year's harvest. Make this drying frame so you too can save seeds!

MEDIUM

Adult Help Needed

WHAT YOU'LL NEED

2 small cardboard boxes with 10×10-inch bottoms
Pencil
Yardstick
Craft knife (adult use only)
Piece of nylon screen cloth
Colored plastic tape
White paper
Clear tape
Clear vinyl adhesive paper

To make 2 shallow boxes, measure and mark 1 inch up from the bottom of each box on all 4 corners. Connect the marks using the yardstick to help you make straight lines. On the bottom of 1 box, measure and mark 1 inch in from all the sides. This will make a rectangular opening. Ask an adult to use the craft knife to cut the boxes along the sides and the opening on the bottom of 1 box. The box with the opening is the frame.

Cut a rectangle of screen cloth 1 inch longer and 1 inch wider than the rectangular opening of the frame. Lay the screen over the opening on the inside of the frame. Tape the screen in place with plastic tape (stretch the screen tightly as you tape). Tape a piece of white paper to inside bottom of the other box with clear tape. This box is the seed box.

Cover both the frame and the seed box with clear adhesive vinyl paper, leaving only the screen and white paper uncovered. Cut 2 triangles out of scraps of cardboard. Place 1 in each of 2 opposite corners of the seed box, and tape them into position with strips of the vinyl adhesive paper.

To use the frame: Set the frame section on top of the seed box with the screen side down. Place dead flower heads or seedpods on the screen. As the flowers and seedpods dry, the seeds will fall through the screen to the white paper in the seed box. Note: This sifter works only for small seeds—ones that can fit through the screen. But you can use the frame as a drying frame for plants with larger seeds.

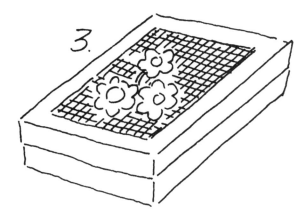

Butterfly Colors

Hoping to attract more butterflies to your garden? Then be sure to use colorful plants. Butterflies actually see more colors than humans can! They seem to prefer red, orange, yellow, purple, and dark pink. A large, colorful garden is easy for butterflies to find, and it encourages them to stay awhile!

SPRING LANTERNS

*Each spring a lantern festival takes place in Taiwan and is
widely celebrated by families. Make a few, or many,
lanterns, and have your own festival.*

WHAT YOU'LL NEED

Aluminum foil
Glue
8¹/₂×11-inch
   construction
   paper
Ruler
Pencil
Scissors
Stapler and staples
   or tape
String or yarn

Glue aluminum foil to 1 side of a piece of construction paper. When the glue is dry, fold the paper in half lengthwise, with the aluminum foil on the inside. Measure and mark lines on the fold side of the paper. Marks should stop 2 inches before the open edge of the paper, and they should be about 1 inch in from each side. Cut on the lines to make slits. Open up the paper, staple or tape the top corners (marked A on the illustration) together, then the bottom corners (marked B on the illustration). Tape string or yarn to the lantern for hanging.

Make many lanterns, and hang them in your backyard to celebrate the coming of spring. Maybe hang them for your first backyard barbeque of the season!

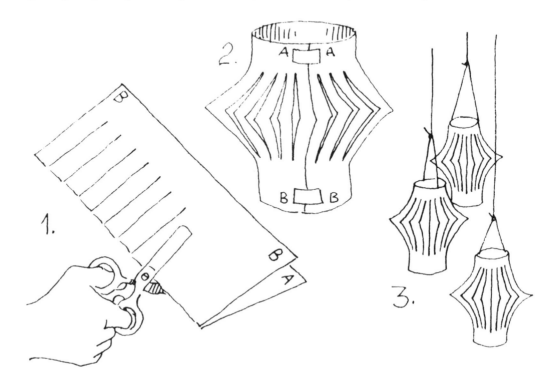

LITTLE WORRY DOLLS

Send your worries away by making miniature dolls who will do all your worrying for you!

WHAT YOU'LL NEED

Aluminum foil
Masking tape
Newspaper
Flour
Water
Large mixing bowl
Measuring cup
Plastic wrap
Gesso (available at an
    art or craft
    store)
Paintbrush
Paints

Follow this Central American tradition, and keep a set of worry dolls under your pillow. Each night before going to sleep, whisper a worry to each doll. After your troubles have been told, as the tradition goes, you can forget about them. The dolls will do all the worrying that's needed!

To make the dolls, mold the basic body shape for each doll out of aluminum foil. You can mold the body in 1 piece or create separate body parts and then attach them using masking tape. When the doll's shape is finished, cover the whole surface of the doll with masking tape. Now the dolls are ready for papier-mâché.

Cover your work surface with newspaper. Tear other sheets of newspaper into small, thin strips, and set aside. Make a thick paste out of flour and water in the mixing bowl; mix 1 cup of flour for every cup of water. Dip the newspaper strips into the paste, and run the strips through your fingers to get rid of excess paste. Lay the strips over the dolls. Cover each doll completely by overlapping the newspaper strips. Set the dolls on newspaper, and let them dry for a day. Then cover them with a second coat of newspaper strips, and set them to dry again. (Keep the paste covered with plastic between uses.) When the dolls are fully dry, paint them with gesso. Let them dry again for about 15 minutes. Now paint the dolls in the colors of your choice. Let them dry completely.

Now it's time to tell them all your troubles!

HAWAIIAN HULA SKIRT

You can learn to dance the hula, but it just doesn't look right unless you have a "grass" skirt. Make this simple skirt, and start dancing!

EASY

WHAT YOU'LL NEED
Rope
Scissors
Green raffia

Measure the rope around your waist and add a few extra inches. Cut the rope this size. Take a piece of green raffia, and hang it from the rope so the ends are even. Tie a knot to hold the raffia in place. Keep adding and tying pieces of raffia onto the rope until it looks like a grass skirt. When the rope is covered (except for the extra inches), tie it around your waist.

Now it's time for hula dancing! The hula is a dance with hand movements that tell a story. You may not have classes in your area to learn how to dance the hula, but you can make up your own stories. Act them out with your hands, and move your body in a rhythmic pattern.

Teach a few of your friends your new-style hula, and put on a show for the neighborhood or your families!

Dancing With Flowers
Hawaiian hula dancers often wear leis, braided or woven necklaces made of natural material such as flowers or shells. That's because the lei is the traditional offering to Laka, goddess of the dance. Leis are also given to people when they visit Hawaii to symbolize friendship.

MILITARY DOG TAGS

These dog tags aren't for dogs! They're ID tags like the metal ones American soldiers wear. Cool!

DIFFICULT

Adult Help Needed

WHAT YOU'LL NEED

Pencil *or* pen
Aluminum pie pan
Ruler
Work gloves
Heavy-duty scissors
Needle-nose pliers
Paper clip
Hole punch
18 inches of ball
  chain

You must have an adult help you with this project. Use a pencil or pen point to mark two 1½×2¼-inch rectangles on the flat portion of the pie tin. Wearing work gloves, cut out the tags with scissors. Trim the corners of the tags diagonally to make a pair of octagons.

Have an adult use the pliers to bend back the edges of the tags about ⅛ inch. Fold corners first, then tops and bottoms, and then the sides. Again wearing your work gloves, place each tag right-side up on a hard surface and use the ruler to gently smooth the edges of the tags by rubbing the ruler along all the folded-down edges. (Have the adult check to make sure there are no sharp edges remaining.)

Now it's time to emboss your initials on the tags with the end of a paper clip. Place the tags on a soft surface, such as a stack of newspaper, and use just enough pressure to raise the letters without poking through the aluminum. Punch a hole in each tag ¼ inch from the top.

String your tags, back sides together, onto the ball chain. Wear your tags with pride!

Honor Medal

Millions of American soldiers wear metal identification tags, but only a select few have worn the Medal of Honor. Since the medal's creation in 1861, only 3,400 men and women have received this top award for heroic action in our nation's battles!

JAPANESE PAPER DOLL

For Hina Matsuri (March 3), make Japanese paper dolls
that wear traditional kimonos. In Japan, this day
is devoted to dolls.

**WHAT YOU'LL
NEED**
Poster board
Ruler
Scissors
Construction paper
Markers or colored
    pencils
Tape

From poster board, cut out a rectangle that measures 7×2 inches tall. At a
short end of the rectangle, cut out a round head shape. Trim below the head to
make sloping shoulders. (This should look like a large, round-headed clothespin.)

For the kimono, cut out a 6-inch square from colored construction paper. For
the sash, cut out a 6×⅜-inch rectangle from black paper. Cut out a wig from the
black paper. In the center of the wig, cut a horizontal slit that is wide enough to
fit over the doll's head. Fit the wig onto the doll's head.

With markers or pen-
cils, draw a face on the
doll. Fold down the top
⅜ inch of the kimono to
make a collar. Color the
collar with a marker or
pencil. Lay the kimono
flat so the folded collar is
facedown.

slit →

1.

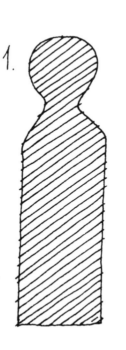

2.

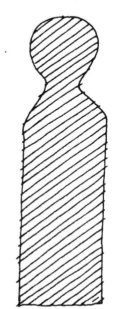

Center the body on top of the kimono. Fold a top corner of the kimono down over the doll's shoulder. Working on the same side of the kimono, fold the paper vertically to cover the doll's body. Use the same method to fold the opposite side of the kimono. Wrap the sash around the doll from front to back, and tape the ends together in the back.

Make dolls for your friends or to decorate your table for a special March 3 tea party! You don't have to be in Japan to celebrate dolls!

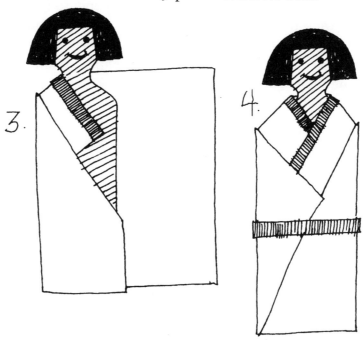

A Girl's First Doll

Japanese paper dolls were originally charms, made of straw or paper, that were placed near babies to protect them from childhood diseases. On Hina Matsuri, or Girl's Day, people floated dolls down rivers, believing the dolls would carry away illness and misfortune. It is traditional today in Japan for a girl to receive one of these dolls on the occasion of her first Hina Matsuri.

PAPER GONDOLA

In Venice, Italy, these boats are used just like we use taxis
in the United States. Make a miniature gondola,
and display it in your room.

**WHAT YOU'LL
NEED**
Black construction
   paper
Scissors
Glue
Gold fadeless or
   origami paper
Glitter
Construction paper
Tape

Fold a piece of black construction paper in quarters, then, with the open fold on the left, cut out the bow shape (see illustration). Unfold the paper, then glue the ends together to create the bow and stern.

To create the beak, fold the gold paper in half, draw a design similar to the one shown, and cut it out. Glue it to one end of the gondola. Draw a decorative line with glue on the side of the boat, and sprinkle the glue with glitter.

To make the gondola stand, fold a 2×8-inch strip of construction paper in half. Cut a notch in the center that is 1 inch wide at the top and 1 inch deep. Tape the ends together and set your gondola into the notch.

Buon viaggio!

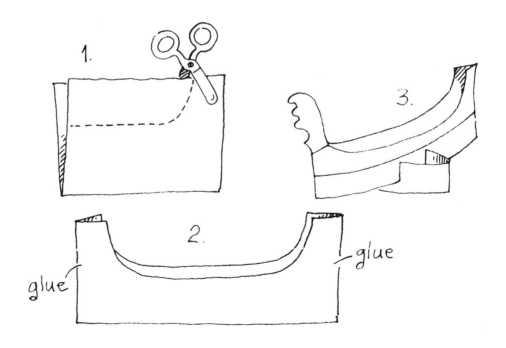

CHILI-PEPPER GOOD LUCK CHARM (RISTRA)

Make this colorful Ristra with paper chilies, and hang it in your doorway as a good luck charm and welcome sign.

WHAT YOU'LL NEED

Construction paper
Pencil
Scissors
Hole punch
24 inches of twine
Glue (optional)

Cut out about 24 peppers in small (2½ inches long), medium (4¼ inches long), and large (5¼ inches long) shapes. Make some peppers yellow, some red, some green, and others orange—be sure you have a good variety of colors and sizes.

Punch a hole in each pepper through the stem. Fold the twine in half, leave a loop at the top, and make a knot. String on the peppers, alternating colors and sizes. Knot the twine after every 2 or 3 peppers. When you're done tying on all the peppers, hang your good luck charm on your bedroom door to welcome your friends.

If you'd like to make more realistic looking peppers, turn to page 131. Read the instructions given for stuffing the bread. To "stuff" your peppers, double the number of peppers you cut out, and follow the directions given. After your peppers are stuffed, follow the directions above to string the peppers.

Hot, hot, hot!

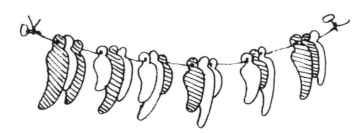

WHAT A DOLL

Cornhusk dolls were made by Native Americans in what is now the northeastern United States. Here's how you can make one.

DIFFICULT

WHAT YOU'LL NEED
Cornhusks
String
Scissors
Markers
Dried flowers
(optional)

1. Strip the husks from several ears of corn. Let them dry out for a few days. Make the doll's head by rolling up 1 husk into a ball. Put another cornhusk over the rolled-up husk, and use string to tie this piece tightly under the rolled-up husk.

2. Roll a husk lengthwise to make the arms. Tie the roll at each end. Put this roll under the head, and use string to hold the arms in place.

3. Use several husks to make a skirt. Lay these husks in the front and back of the arms, and tie the husks below the arms to hold them in place. Trim the bottom of the skirt with scissors so it is even.

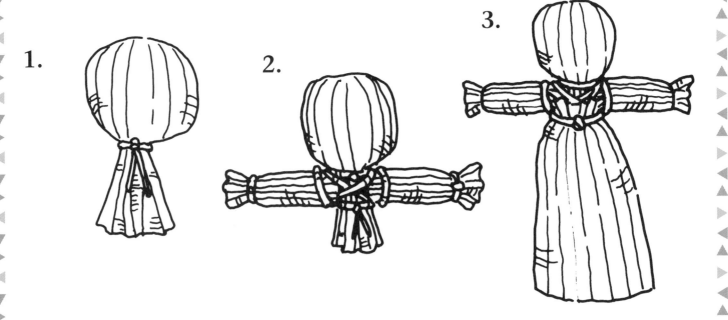

1.

2.

3.

4. To make the blouse, cut a rectangle out of a husk. On a long side of the rectangle, make a cut halfway through to the other side. Put the rectangle behind the doll, with the cut end up. The end of the rectangle that is not cut will be the back of the blouse. Fold the cut end of the rectangle over to the front of the doll. This will be the front of the blouse. Cross the flaps over each other, and use string to tie the blouse in place.

5. Finally, draw a face on your cornhusk doll. You can put dried flowers in its hand or make a bonnet for its head out of cornhusks.

4.

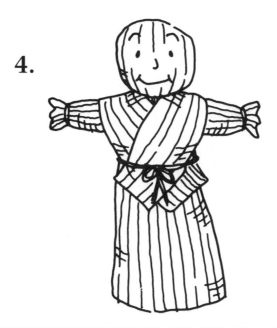

Corn Cure

Corn has been an important crop associated with Native Americans for
many centuries. But did you know that many tribes used corn in medicines?
The Cherokee nation used the vegetable as a ceremonial medicine as well as in
a green corn medicine used to treat many common ailments.

DREAM CATCHER

Make all your good dreams come true!

DIFFICULT

Adult Help Needed

WHAT YOU'LL NEED

Plastic coffee can lid
Scissors
Ribbon
Craft glue
Embroidery thread
Needle
Beads
Thin leather cord, twine, or heavy string
Feathers

Cut out the middle of a plastic coffee can lid, leaving just the ring; ask an adult to help you with this part. Wind the ribbon several times around the ring until it is totally covered and nicely padded; glue the ends in place.

Loosely wrap embroidery thread around the plastic ring to form 8 loops. Cut the end of the thread and tie the 2 ends together so they are on the back of the ring. Use a needle and another piece of embroidery thread to weave the thread in and out of the loops around the ring. Loosely knot the thread to each loop. Then sew each loop with its opposite loop to make a web. Hold a bead in the center, and pass the thread through it each time you sew 2 loops together.

To finish, tie 2 lengths of leather cord to the bottom of the ring; the cords should hang down 4 or 5 inches. Thread beads on the cord, and knot the cord ends to hold the beads. Glue feathers to the ends of the cords.

Hang the dream catcher over your bed. All your bad dreams will get caught in the web, but all your good dreams will pass through the center and come true!

DREAM CATCHER

In an old American Indian legend about the origin of the dream catcher, a Native American girl was shown in a dream how a spider spins her web. The girl was then shown how to weave the web into a dream catcher. When she woke the next morning, colorful beads dangled from a real dream catcher to represent the good dreams she had during the night!

CODED MESSAGE KITES

Make an easy kite to send a coded message to a friend.

WHAT YOU'LL NEED

Permanent markers
Plastic shopping bag
Ball of string
Ribbon
Stapler and staples

With the markers, draw some pictures on the plastic bag to make a coded message for a friend to read when the kite is in the air. Tie the handles of the plastic shopping bag together with the end of a ball of string. Staple a few 2-foot lengths of ribbon to the bottom of the bag for kite tails.

Find a windy spot outdoors (away from any overhead wires), and start running. As the bag fills with air, slowly let out the string. The kite should begin to soar and dive. See if your friend can figure out the message you drew on the kite.

Don't forget to take your kite in the house or put it in a trash can when you've finished playing with it—plastic bags are dangerous for small children and animals.

Ancient Kites

Kites may be just for fun nowadays, but back around 1200 B.C. (when they were invented in China) they were used to send coded messages between military camps.

NEW YEAR'S GARLAND

Make these lacy garlands out of colored paper, and string them up in your home when it's time to celebrate the New Year.

MEDIUM

WHAT YOU'LL NEED
Colored construction paper or tissue paper
Scissors
Craft glue or glue stick

Cut out twelve 4-inch circles from colored paper. Fold each circle in half, in half again, and, finally, in half a third time. It should now look like a slice of pie. Cut out a series of small snips from both folded edges. Unfold the snipped circles.

Apply glue along the edge of a circle. (If you are using construction paper, use craft glue; if you are using tissue paper, use a glue stick). Place a second circle on top of the first so that the edges stick together. Apply glue to the center of the second circle, and place a third circle on top of it. Continue adding the remaining circles, alternately gluing the edges and the centers. When the glue is dry, gently pull the top and bottom circle in opposite directions.

Hang the stretched garland for your New Year's celebration!

Celebrating the New Year

People in the United States celebrate the New Year by throwing confetti into the air. In China, long, lacy garlands decorate the streets for New Year.

CULTURES OF THE WORLD BOOK

Learn more about people of another culture, and recognize more about yourself at the same time.

MEDIUM

WHAT YOU'LL NEED

Reference material (encyclopedias, Internet access, personal interviews)
Cereal box
Scissors
$8\frac{1}{2}\times11$-inch white paper
Hole punch
Ribbon or string
Photos and/or magazine pictures
Markers
Construction paper or contact paper
Glue

Each page on the left-hand side of this book will contain a picture and some information about people from another culture. Right-hand pages will have a picture and some information about you or someone from your culture. Don't just limit your information to what is different about you and a child from another culture; try to also find things you have in common!

You might want to have a theme for your book, such as food, clothing, or music. (Your teacher might want to have a World's Fair Day and have each student make one of these books. Then the class will have information about many different cultures.) Do your research to decide what you want to put in your book.

To make a book, cut a $9\frac{1}{2}\times6$-inch rectangle from the cereal box and place it picture-side up. Fold it in half, matching the 6-inch sides together. Stack 4 sheets of white paper, fold the sheets into quarters, cut along the top, and place the paper inside the folded cardboard. Punch 3 holes along the folded edge, through the paper and cardboard, and thread the ribbon through the holes. Tie the ribbon to bind the book.

Decorate the outside of the book with markers or cover it with construction paper. Now fill your book with all your information!

STICK PICTURE FRAMES

In the early days of the United States, picture frames might have looked like these. But these probably smell better!

WHAT YOU'LL NEED

Cinnamon sticks
Raffia or twine
Craft paper, parchment, or burlap
Scissors
Craft glue
Photograph
Picture hanger or soda-can pop top

Tie 4 cinnamon sticks together at the corners with raffia or twine. To make the background, cut out craft paper, parchment, or burlap to fit the size of the frame. Glue the edges of the backing to the back of the cinnamon sticks. Carefully cut your photograph to fit inside the frame; you can make it smaller than the inside of the frame. Center and glue the picture inside the frame. Glue a picture hanger or metal soda-can pop top to the back of the frame for hanging.

A Spicy Tree

Do you know how cinnamon is made? It comes from the dried bark of a tree. The waste and other parts of the bark are called oil of cinnamon, which is used as a flavoring and has also been used in medicines. Cinnamon was a favorite spice in biblical times, when it was used for perfume and incense.

TINGMIUJANG (ESKIMO GAME)

Use clay to make pieces for this game Eskimo children play to help pass the long, cold winters of the Arctic.

WHAT YOU'LL NEED

Air-dry paper clay
Large piece of
    brown craft
    paper or vinyl
Scissors

Use the clay to make 15 birds, about 1 inch long, in the shape of a duck with a simple head and beak, a pointed tail, and a flat bottom (they must have flat bottoms for the game to work). Air dry the clay overnight or until dry.

For a playing cloth, cut a piece of vinyl or brown craft paper in the shape of an animal pelt. Lay the pelt on the floor, and have your friends sit around it.

Now it's time to play the game! The first player shakes the birds in her or his hands and tosses them up gently so they fall on the cloth. Some will land upright; others will fall on their sides. Each upright bird is taken by the player its beak points to. The next player shakes and tosses the remaining birds. Again, the upright birds are claimed by the person they face. The game continues until all the birds have been claimed. The player with the most birds wins.

MAGNETS DE MAYO

These colorful flowers are actually made of corn and beans!

Green, white, and red are the colors of the Mexican flag, and you can combine them in lots of interesting ways when you paint the corn and beans that make up these flower magnets.

Choose an assortment of dried beans to vary the shapes of your flowers. Tiny lentils and corn kernels will make delicate posies, while larger fava beans can become the leaves of a gorgeous bloom. Paint lots of dried beans and corn in the colors of Mexico, and let them dry. Then arrange 6 to 10 beans and kernels in a flower shape. Place the points of the corn kernels toward the center of the flower.

Cut a circle of felt a bit larger than your flower. Cover the circle with glue, and arrange your flower on it. Put the felt flower on waxed paper, and cover the flower completely with glue. If some of the glue runs over the edges of your flower, don't worry. You can break off the extra glue when it is dry.

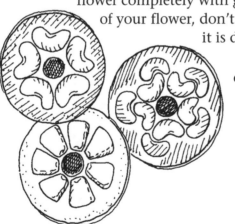

When your flower is completely dry, peel it off the waxed paper and press a piece of sticky-backed magnetic strip on the back.

Mexican Independence Day
Cinco de Mayo is a holiday celebrated on May 5 by Mexicans and Mexican Americans. The holiday is a celebration of freedom and liberty honoring Mexico's victory over the French army in 1862. Many people think of Cinco de Mayo as Mexico's Independence Day—just like July 4 is U.S.A.'s Independence Day!

CAVE PAINTINGS

Make a cave painting—it may bring you luck!

EASY

WHAT YOU'LL NEED

Brown paper
   grocery bag or
   brown paper
Pencil
Scratch paper
Wide black marker
   or charcoal
   (optional)
Paintbrush
Black and earth-
   toned tempera
   paints (red,
   orange, brown,
   gold)

Some people who lived in caves painted on the walls of the caves. Most of their pictures were of buffalo, deer, and other wild animals because people thought these drawings would bring them good luck when hunting.

Prepare the surface of the bag so it looks rough and worn—crinkle the paper, spray it with water in the sink (don't soak it), then let it dry completely. Using a pencil and scratch paper, make a few sample sketches of animals you would like to include in your painting. You don't need to include every detail—make your creatures from simple shapes, such as circles, triangles, and rectangles. Don't worry if your animals don't look exactly like those in photographs, neither do the original cave paintings.

Once you're happy with your sketch, you're ready to draw on the brown paper. After making a rough pencil sketch on the bag, go over the pencil marks with black paint, marker, or charcoal, making sure the lines are thick and strong. Add details, such as eyes, ears, horns, tails, or antlers. When the black lines have dried, paint the figure and background with earth-toned paints.

For more fun, make up a story about your cave painting!

AFRICAN MUD PAINTINGS

Decorate greeting cards for family and friends using mud paint, which is how the Senufo people in Africa paint designs on fabric!

EASY

WHAT YOU'LL NEED

½ cup dirt
Kitchen strainer
Disposable container
½ cup poster paint
   (blue or black will
   look authentic)
Stirring stick
Newspaper
Unbleached muslin
Black felt-tip pen
Toothbrush
Small paintbrush

Optional: Pencil,
   construction
   paper, craft glue

This project can be quite messy. Be sure you have adult permission to do this project inside. It is a good outside project in warm weather!

Put the dirt in the strainer, and set it on top of the disposable container. Slowly run water over the dirt, and let the mud run through the strainer into the container. Once all the dirt has been strained, let the container sit until the mud sinks to the bottom (probably overnight). Pour off the extra water. Mix the paint into the mud.

Cover your work area with newspaper. Smooth out a small piece of muslin. With the black felt-tip pen, draw a picture or design on the fabric (you might want to try sketching it first with a pencil). With a toothbrush, fill in the large areas of your design with the mud paint. Paint patterns, lines, or dots with the small paintbrush. Let the painting dry. You can frame your picture or just hang it on the wall.

You can also make greeting cards, stationery, or placemats by gluing the dried painting onto construction paper. Think of other cool projects you can come up with for this painting technique!

ALOHA HAWAIIAN LEI

Make your own version of the colorful lei Hawaiians give visitors as a way of saying "aloha" or "welcome." Theirs are made of beautiful flowers, but these will last longer.

WHAT YOU'LL NEED

Uncooked ziti pasta
Tempera paints
Paintbrush
Waxed paper
Colored crepe paper
Scissors
String
Large sewing needle

Color 16 pieces of uncooked ziti using tempera paints. Let them dry on waxed paper. Cut out bunches of flower shapes from colored crepe paper. Loosely tie a knot in one end of a 3-foot piece of string. Thread the other end through the eye of a large sewing needle. Sew through the centers of a dozen or so flowers. String on a piece of painted ziti. Continue sewing on flowers and pasta, stopping 3 inches from the end of the string. Undo the beginning knot, and tie the string ends together with a knot (be sure the lei is long enough to fit over your head). Aloha!

Lei Day

In Hawaii, Don Blanding, a poet and artist, noticed that most leis were being worn by tourists rather than the islanders who made them. So, on May 1, 1928, the first Lei Day was instituted. The following year Lei Day became an official holiday, and every year islanders adorn themselves with leis!

LION MASK

On the third day of the Chinese New Year the Lion
Dance begins. Some people believe putting money
in the lion's mouth will bring them luck!

MEDIUM

WHAT YOU'LL NEED

Newspaper
Paper plate
Scissors
Stapler
2 paper egg-carton
  sections
Tape
White glue
Water
Measuring cup
Large mixing bowl
Spoon
Tempera paint
Paintbrush
Beads
Sequins
Feathers
Ribbon scraps

1. Cover your work surface with newspaper. Cut a slit in each side of the paper plate. Pull the edges of each slit together, and overlap them. Staple the edges together. This will bend the plate into a face shape.

2. Tape on the egg-carton sections for bulgy eyes. Make a fist-size ball of newspaper, and tape it in place for the lion's snout. Crumple up some newspaper, and put it under the mask so it will keep its form while you work.

3. Tear 7 to 8 newspaper pages into strips. Mix ½ cup white glue with ½ cup water in a large mixing bowl. Soak the newspaper strips in the glue/water mixture. When you take the strips out of the mixture, run them between your fingers to remove the excess liquid. Cover the mask front with a layer of newspaper strips. Let the mask dry overnight.

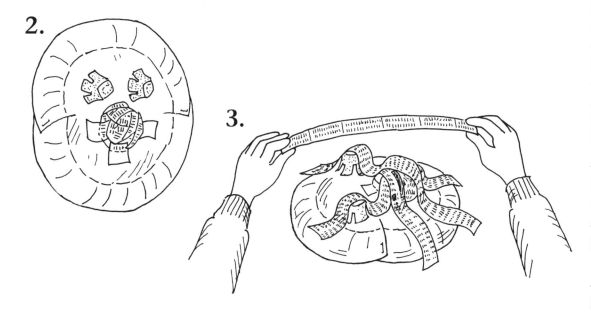

4. Add a second layer of strips; smooth the strips over the mask with your fingers. Let the mask dry overnight.

5. Paint the mask with 2 coats of red tempera paint. Let dry.

6. Paint on the lion's mouth; decorate the mask with beads, sequins, and feathers. Tape a loop of ribbon to the back of the mask to hang it on your wall.

6.

New Year's Chores

Chinese children don't do chores on Chinese New Year's Day. Sweeping or dusting on New Year's Day is believed to be sweeping away good fortune. Children, as well as close friends and relatives, are given *lai see*, little red envelopes with a crisp bill inside, for good fortune.

BALLOON FORTUNES

People of different cultures have different methods for telling fortunes. The Chinese put paper fortunes in cookies. Create your own fortune-telling method!

WHAT YOU'LL 👓👓 NEED 👓👓

Construction paper
Hole punch
Balloons
Funnel
Paper
Marker or pen
Pins

Punch circles out of brightly colored construction paper with a hole punch. Stuff as many circles or confetti pieces as you can into each deflated balloon using a funnel.

Write fortunes on small pieces of paper, and slip them into the balloons. Blow up the balloons (keep your head down while blowing so you don't inhale any confetti), and hang them high but within reach.

During a party or other fun time, hand out pins and let everyone pop a balloon and read their fortune. (Warn people there will be popping balloons before starting this game—some children are afraid of the sound.) And the flying confetti is fun too!

(Balloons are choking hazards. After popping the balloons, immediately pick up all the balloon pieces to keep them away from young children.)

EID UL-FITR CARDS

Eid ul-Fitr is an important Muslim festival, during which people give each other presents and cards. The Muslim religion forbids the drawing of people or animals, so these cards are decorated with beautiful designs made from geometric shapes and patterns.

MEDIUM

Adult Help Needed

WHAT YOU'LL NEED

Cardboard
Heavy-duty scissors
Pencil
Chenille stems
Glue brush
Craft glue
Paintbrush
Paints
Scrap paper
Light-colored construction paper

Cut a 3-inch square of cardboard with the heavy-duty scissors (you may need adult help with this part). On the cardboard, make a rough pencil sketch of the pattern you want to print. Twist the chenille stems into the shapes that make up your pattern. Brush a thin layer of glue onto your cardboard pattern. While the glue is wet, press the chenille stem shapes onto the design. Let the glue dry completely.

Use a paintbrush to apply paint to the raised pattern on your cardboard (this is your printing block). Place the printing block on top of a piece of scrap paper, and gently press down on the block. Carefully pull the block away from the paper to see the printed pattern. Practice printing on the scrap paper a few times before printing your designs on folded sheets of construction paper to make cards.

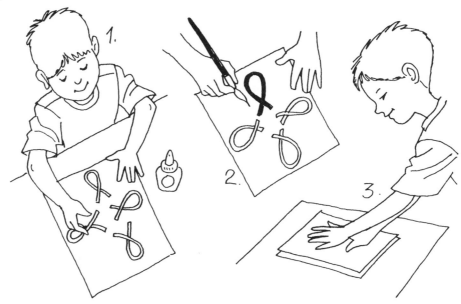

PARROT PIÑATA

A piñata is a decorated container filled with sweet treats. You hit the piñata with a stick. When it bursts, everyone gathers the goodies.

DIFFICULT

Adult Help Needed

WHAT YOU'LL
👀 NEED 👀
Newspaper
12-inch balloon
Flour
Water
Large mixing bowl
Measuring cup
Spoon
Scissors
Ruler
Nail
Poster paints
Paintbrush
Poster board
Markers
Masking tape
Colored tissue paper
Craft glue
Assorted candy
Strong string

1. Cover your work surface with newspaper. Blow up the balloon, and knot the end. Make a paste by mixing 1 cup of flour for each cup of water in a large mixing bowl. Blend the paste until it is smooth. Cut 7 or 8 pages of newspaper into 1×4-inch strips. Dip a strip of newspaper in the paste. Run the strip between your fingers to remove excess paste. Place the strip over the balloon and smooth in place. Continue covering the balloon with a layer of strips, overlapping them slightly. Then apply 3 more layers of strips. Let the balloon dry for a few days—keep turning the balloon so all parts of it dry thoroughly. Once dry, use a nail to carefully poke 2 small holes at the top about 4 inches apart.

2. Paint the balloon body in bright colors. Let the paint dry. Draw a parrot head shape and 2 wing shapes on a piece of poster board. Color them in, and add details with markers. Cut the shapes from the poster board, and tape them to the balloon body with masking tape. Dab paint over the tape to conceal it. Cut long strips of colored tissue paper for the parrot's tail. Glue the tissue paper strips to the balloon body.

Cover balloon with strips.

Cut out parrot head and wings.

3. With an adult's help, cut a 3-inch-wide triangular flap between the 2 top holes. Fold back the flap to remove the balloon, and fill the piñata with candy. To make the hanger, thread a piece of string through the 2 top holes and knot the ends. Push the flap back in place. Now you're ready to have plenty of piñata fun with your friends!

Cut a triangular flap to fill the piñata with candy.

It's Raining Food

There are several stories about the origin of the piñata. One legend has it that the first piñata was a clay pot decorated to look like a cloud in honor of Tlaloc, the Rain God. When it was broken, it showered down food and good things to the ground, much as the rain brought crops and flowers to the people.

AFRICAN TUTSI BASKET

Small baskets like these are made by the Tutsi people of Africa.
Now make your own with construction paper!

WHAT YOU'LL 👀 NEED 👀

2 sheets 9×12-inch
  red construction
  paper
Ruler
Pencil
Scissors
3 sheets 9×12-inch
  beige construc-
  tion paper
Craft glue
5-inch plate
Clear tape
9-inch plate

The Tutsi people of Africa make these baskets by coiling long strands of dried grass around and around, binding them together with thinner strands. The baskets have lids and are used to hold grain. Hold your treasures in your basket!

Cut 8 strips of red construction paper, each 12 inches long and ¾ inch wide. With 2 pieces of the beige construction paper, glue the 12-inch-long edges of the pieces together (overlap the edges a little). After the glue has dried, cut 4 strips 16 inches long and ½ inch wide.

Glue 2 red strips together at the middle to form a cross (see step 1). Do this with all the other red strips until you have 4 red crosses. Place the 4 crosses on top of each other, and fan them out evenly. Glue them in place—they should look like a star (see step 2).

Use the 5-inch plate to draw a circle on the other piece of red construction paper. Cut out the circle, and glue it to the center of the star. This forms the bottom of your basket. Fold the rays of the star up at the edge of the circle (see step 3).

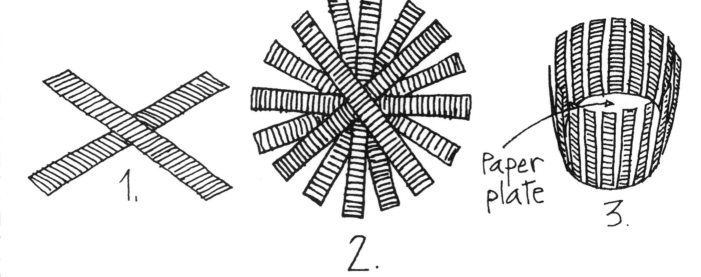

Paper plate

1.

2.

3.

Tape a beige strip horizontally across the bottom of 1 ray. Weave the beige strip over and under the rays all the way around (see step 4). Remove the tape, and glue the ends of the beige strip together. Hold ends together until glue begins to dry. Repeat with remaining beige strips. Push beige strips close together before gluing.

After you've finished weaving the beige strips, fold over and glue the red ends to the inside of the basket, forming a rim. Make a pointed lid for the basket by using the 9-inch plate to trace a circle on the last sheet of beige construction paper. Cut out the circle, then cut a pie wedge out of the circle (the bigger the wedge, the taller the lid) (see step 5). Overlap and glue the cut ends together. (Note: If you don't want to use red and beige paper, use any 2 colors you'd like.)

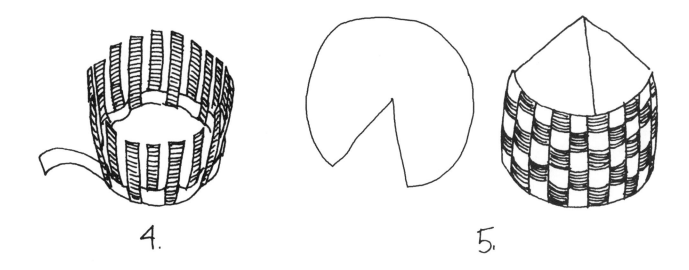

4.

5.

Tall People, Small Baskets

Baskets made by the Tutsi people of central Africa may be small, but the Tutsi people are among the tallest in the world. In fact, the Tutsi are often more than 7 feet in height. The Tutsi live in round grass huts scattered throughout the hilly countryside.

NATIVE AMERICAN NOISEMAKER

All children, no matter their nationality or culture,
love a good noisemaker!

**WHAT YOU'LL
NEED**
2-inch coat button
with 2 holes
Brown poster paint
Paintbrush
2 small pegs or sticks
20 inches waxed
string or cord

You've probably used noisemakers at parties. But I'll bet you didn't know Native American children used to play with noisemakers that hummed and buzzed—all without electronics! Now you can make one of these fun toys, too.

Paint the large coat button so it looks like clay. Then paint the pegs or sticks. Thread the waxed string or cord through both holes in the button, and tie the ends together. Place the end loops of the cord around the pegs or sticks to make handles. Wind handles in opposite directions until the cord is very twisted. To make the toy hum or buzz, pull the handles apart so the cord untwists. The button will spin, bob up and down, and make a noise!

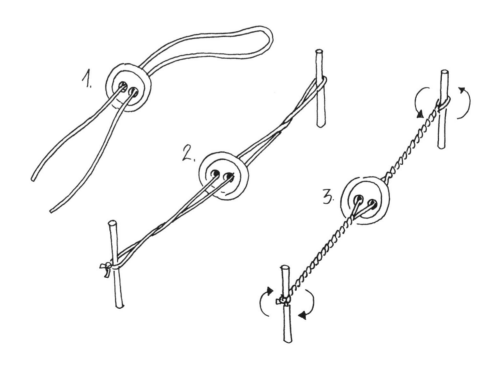

HINDU RANGOLI PATTERN

During the Diwali festival, rangoli patterns, made with colored flour paste, rice, and spices, decorate the entrance to many Hindu homes. You can make a rangoli pattern with glitter.

WHAT YOU'LL NEED

Newspaper
Paper
Pencil
Glue
Paintbrush (optional)
Different colors of
   glitter

Since this project is very messy, first cover your work surface with lots of old newspaper. Draw a fancy design in pencil on a piece of paper. Carefully paint or squeeze a thin line of glue over some parts of the pencil design. Sprinkle 1 color of glitter over the line of glue. To remove excess glitter from the design, carefully tip your glitter design onto another piece of paper and shake off the excess glitter. Make a small paper funnel, and put excess glitter back into the tube. Continue adding several different colors of glitter to your design this way. Let the glued glitter dry completely before you hang your colorful creation.

If you'd like to be more authentic, try using powdered cinnamon, nutmeg, ginger, cloves, uncooked rice, or pasta for your design. (Be sure to ask adult permission before using these supplies!) Apply them to your design on the paper just as you would the glitter.

NAVAJO GROANING STICK

Navajo dancers used these pieces of wood on a whip to make the sound of great winds and distant thunder.

MEDIUM

Adult Help Needed

WHAT YOU'LL NEED
- Lightweight wood (like a shingle or part of a fruit or vegetable crate)
- Small saw
- Ruler
- Drill or hammer and large nail
- 3 feet of heavy twine
- Scissors
- Poster paints
- Paintbrushes

(Adult supervision advised when using the Groaning Stick!)

Ask an adult to help you cut a piece of lightweight wood 2×6 inches. About 1 inch from a 2-inch side of the piece of wood, have an adult help you drill a hole in the center of the wood or hammer in a large nail (carefully, so the wood doesn't split) to make a hole. If using a nail, remove the nail when the hole is made. Thread 1 end of heavy twine through the hole. Tie the twine to the wood with several tight knots (ask an adult to make sure the knots are secure).

Hold the piece of wood at the point where the string is attached. Measure the string from your outstretched arm to your opposite shoulder, and cut the twine that length. Paint your groaning stick with designs—Navajo symbols such as the thunderbird, lightning, rain, and clouds look nice. Let the paint dry completely.

To use the stick, wrap some of the twine around your right hand (or your left hand, if you are left-handed). Lift your hand (wrapped in twine) over your head, and swing the groaning stick around. After a few turns it should start to hum and buzz. If not, try adjusting the length of the twine.

Always be careful when you stop spinning the stick. Lower your arm slowly, keeping it outstretched in front of you so it doesn't hit you. Also, always use your groaning stick away from people and other objects!

NATIVE AMERICAN MOCCASINS

In pioneer days, shoes were very expensive and not always easy to obtain. Pioneer families copied the moccasins they saw worn by Native Americans. You can, too!

DIFFICULT

Adult Help Needed

WHAT YOU'LL NEED

Newspaper
Pencil
Ruler
Scissors
Sewing pins
Fabric (such as felt or canvas)
Markers
Embroidery floss
Beads
Heavy-duty sewing needle
Strong thread

Stand barefoot on a piece of newspaper, and trace around 1 foot with a pencil. Then, draw a pattern around the traced foot (as shown in diagram 1). Find the distance from 1 to 2 and from 3 to 4 by measuring across your instep and dividing that number in half. (Ask an adult if you need help with this calculation.)

Pin the pattern on the fabric, trace around it, and cut it out. (If the fabric you are using is very thick, you may need to have an adult cut it for you.) Trace and cut another pattern for your other foot. Decorate the flaps (tops) of the moccasins with markers, embroidered designs, or sewn-on beads (as shown in diagram 2).

Fold 1 moccasin in half, with right sides facing in. Use running stitches to sew the front. Gather the stitches a little to fit the shape of your foot. End with several overlapping stitches. Turn the moccasin right side out, and try it on. Use pins to fit the heel seam, then take the moccasin off. Sew the back seam with running stitches to ¾ inch from the bottom. Trim the seam.

Cut out a small square from the heel (as shown in diagram 3). Flatten the heel, and sew it closed with overcast stitches. For ties, cut 2 strips of fabric, each ½ inch wide and 15 inches long. Then wrap the ties around your ankles just under the top flaps, and tie them in back of the moccasins.

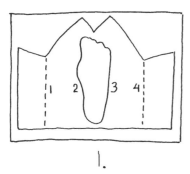

1.

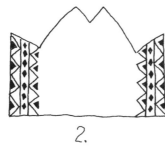

2.

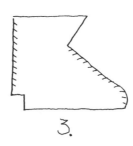

3.

4.

EASY ARTIST'S EASEL

Make these simple easels to display your artwork—you can create your own art gallery!

Adult Help Needed

WHAT YOU'LL NEED

Cardboard box
Tape
Pencil
Yardstick
Heavy-duty scissors
    or craft knife
    (adult use only)
Clothespins

Find a sturdy cardboard box, and tape it shut. On opposite sides, draw a line from the bottom corner to the opposite top corner. Have an adult cut along the diagonals and then across the top and bottom to cut the box in half (see illustration).

Cut 2 small slits at the top of the easel. Attach your artwork by clipping it to the box with the clothespins. You could also use your easel to paint your artwork—just like artists do!

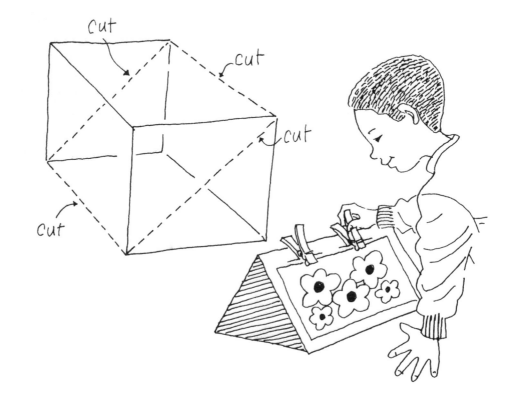

BEADED BEAUTIES

Make your own beautiful sand beads to wear,
just like the ones worn by African women.

MEDIUM

WHAT YOU'LL NEED

Sand
White glue
Spoon
Empty, cleaned
      plastic butter tub
Nail
Foam tray
Markers
Tiny seeds or glitter
Yarn
Tape

Mix sand and glue in the butter tub to make sand dough. Make enough dough to roll a number of beads the size you want. With the nail, poke a hole through the center of the bead. If the dough is too soft to make a hole, add more sand until it is stiff enough to make a hole through the bead. Make lots of beads, then let them dry on a foam tray until they are hard.

When the beads have dried, decorate them by coloring them with markers or gluing tiny seeds or bits of glitter to them. To make a necklace, tape 1 end of a piece of yarn (long enough for a necklace) to the table, and string the beads onto it. Tie the 2 ends of the yarn together when you've strung all your beads.

You've made beautiful beads!

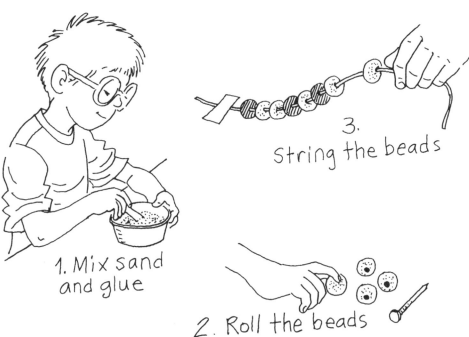

3. String the beads

1. Mix sand and glue

2. Roll the beads

CUTOUT COLLAGE

This *cutout collage* will look like ones made by Henri Matisse,
a famous French painter who created similar designs when arthritis
made it impossible for him to paint in his later years.

**WHAT YOU'LL
NEED**
Colored construc-
tion paper or
tissue paper
Scissors
White or black
construction
paper
Glue

Matisse used geometric and organic (those found in nature) shapes in his compositions. Geometric shapes, such as triangles, circles, and squares, are symmetrical. Organic shapes, on the other hand, or not symmetrical; they include squiggles and blobs.

Begin cutting out shapes in many different sizes and colors from the colored paper. Once you have a collection of shapes, arrange them on a sheet of white or black paper. Glue the cutouts in place. If you made your collage on white paper, mount the work onto black construction paper to create a striking contrast.

COMMUNICATE FOR FUN

Enlarge your world by communicating
with those around you. In this chapter, you'll find
activities that involve a variety of skills: reading,
writing, speaking, and performing. You'll find
ideas to make storybooks, puppets,
scrapbooks, cards, and lots more!

MATCH-UP BOOKS

Create your own collection of kooky characters.

WHAT YOU'LL NEED
2 sheets of white paper (8¹/₂×11 inches)
Scissors
Light cardboard
Crayons or markers
Stapler

Cut each sheet of paper into 3 equal-size rectangles. (Cut across the short side of the paper.) This will give you 6 rectangles. Cut a piece of light cardboard the same size as the rectangles. Stack the 6 paper rectangles on top of each other. Fold them down twice, dividing the papers into 3 sections.

Unfold the rectangles and draw a different person, family member, animal, or monster on each page. Draw the head in the top square, the body in the middle square, and the legs at the bottom. (NOTE: The drawings should all be about the same size, and the heads, bodies, and legs should all line up in the same place. This way the head of one figure will line up with the body on every other drawing.)

After you finish drawing, put the piece of cardboard on the bottom of the stack. Then staple the left side of your drawings together to make a book. Carefully cut across the papers along the folds, stopping before you get to the left side. (Don't cut the cardboard!) Your book is done. Flip through your book, turning different flaps at a time, to see what silly characters you can create!

SHADOW PUPPETS

Put on a shadow puppet show for the neighborhood kids!

MEDIUM

WHAT YOU'LL NEED

Construction paper
Pencil
Scissors
Wooden sticks
Masking tape
Audio cassette and
  tape recorder
  (optional)
Sheet
2 flashlights

With a couple of friends, plan a shadow puppet show to share with your families and other friends. Draw puppet shapes on construction paper, and then cut them out. For Halloween, for example, you might cut out the shapes of a witch, a cat, a ghost, and so on. To do a woodland story, you might cut out simple shapes of a deer, rabbit, bird, and squirrel. Tape each of your puppet shapes onto a wooden stick so they will be easy to hold.

Plan the story you are going to tell, and record it into a tape recorder. You can include background music if you want. Drape a sheet over a doorway. When it is show time, the audience sits on one side of the door while the puppeteers sit on the other side. Turn on the tape. While 2 friends shine flashlights at the draped sheet, the others operate the stick puppets in front of the flashlights. The audience will see the shadows of the puppets on the sheet in the doorway.

Animal Puppets?

Hundreds of years ago in China, shadow puppets were made from the stretched and dried skins of donkeys, sheep, water buffaloes, pigs, and fish, with rods or strings attached to them. Three-dimensional rod puppets evolved from these early shadow puppets.

JOURNAL JAM

Writing in a journal is great fun now, but it will be even more fun to read in a few years!

WHAT YOU'LL NEED

Spiral notebook (plain *colored front* is best)

Pen

Magazines and newspapers

Family pictures

Craft glue

For ages, people have explored their feelings and their ancestry by writing and reading personal journals. Young people, such as World War II's famous heroine Anne Frank, have left behind important messages for future generations.

You can join in this proud tradition by writing your own journal. Once a week, or once a day if you're really anxious to speak your mind, sit down and write out what you've done, what you've seen, and how you feel. Date each page with the month, day, and year. Be sure to mention how much things cost; popular trends; and troubling, interesting, and exciting things you hear about in the news. Glue in family pictures or images from magazines and newspapers to verify what you say.

Five, ten, even a hundred years from now, people could be using your journal to better understand the times in which you lived.

NOTE KEEPER KEEPSAKE

Create a special place to keep special things.

EASY

WHAT YOU'LL NEED

Small wooden or paper box (a shoe box is okay)
Old magazines and newspapers
Photographs
Scissors
Craft glue
Paintbrush

Have you ever found a feather that was so beautiful it took your breath away? Have you ever been given a note that was so sweet you just couldn't throw it away? Well, this special box is the perfect place to keep all those treasures. In fact, it will wind up being a treasure itself.

Go through boxes of family photos, old magazines, and newspapers, and cut out pictures and words that are special to you. (Be sure to get permission before cutting anything!) Glue those pictures on the lid of your keepsake box. With the paintbrush, paint a thin coat of glue over the lid. (Be sure the glue you use will be clear when it dries.)

Your box has become more than just a box—it's a reflection of who you are. And it's the perfect place to keep your most private possessions.

So Many Kisses

The X's that you put at the end of notes to mean kisses were first used in the early 1000s. English lords closed their documents with a cross that they would kiss before signing their names. This meant that they were faithful to God and their king. Over the years, the cross slanted and became an X.

FAMILY NEWSLETTER

Stop the presses! Report on your family's latest news!

MEDIUM

WHAT YOU'LL NEED

Typing paper
Typewriter and copy machine or computer and printer
Postage stamps
Envelopes

Have you ever heard your mother complain about how Aunt Lucy never writes? Does Grandma Jane talk about how your mother never calls? You can bring the whole family together by writing and distributing this fun family newsletter. First, ask your parents for the addresses, birthdays, and anniversaries of all your relatives. Then drop your relatives notes asking them what's been happening in their lives. Once you get your answers, write short reports on each family group and add a reminder box of their special dates. Print out copies for each family, and drop them in the mail. (You can e-mail those that have computers.) Before you know it, you'll be getting announcements from your long-lost Uncle Harold (not to mention thank-you notes from Aunt Lucy who never writes).

DOGGIE DIARY

Can you talk to the animals? Can they talk back?

MEDIUM

WHAT YOU'LL NEED

Notebook
Pen

Some experts say our pets have their own distinctive languages, even if we don't know how to interpret what they say. This fun experiment might help you get a clue to doggy dialogue. The next time you have a free day at home with your dog, pay close attention to how he "talks." Does he whimper when he wants to go outside? Write it down. Does he give a loud, short bark when he's hungry? Make a note of it. Now see if you can duplicate the sounds to communicate with your dog.

FACE CHARADES

*Can you let everyone know how you
feel—without saying anything?*

MEDIUM

**WHAT YOU'LL
NEED**

Pens or pencils
Paper
Cup or hat

This game is a lot like regular charades, but instead of acting out a word or phrase, you act out a feeling or emotion and have the other players guess what it is. This is a great game for the back of the car, where you can't move around much.

Before you begin, have each person write 3 or 4 emotions on different pieces of paper. Fold them up, and put them into a cup or hat. Each player takes a turn drawing an emotion out of the cup and then acting it out for the other players. This must be done without making any sound and without moving any part of the body except for the face and head. That's right—no hand, arm, leg, or other body motions.

The following are some feelings and emotions to start out with. How many more can you think of?

HAPPINESS	SADNESS	SHYNESS	SURPRISE
HUNGER	ANGER	LOVE	CONFUSION
FRIGHT	SLEEPINESS	DISGUST	BOREDOM

Lots and Lots of Words

When you use words to communicate, you have a lot to choose from. The average American's vocabulary is around 10,000 words—15,000 if you are really smart! The famous writer William Shakespeare had a vocabulary of over 29,000 words.

GOURD PUPPETS

Pick out some funny-shaped gourds, make puppets, and put on a show!

DIFFICULT

Adult Help Needed

WHAT YOU'LL NEED

Small gourds
Paint
Paintbrush
Knife
Spoon
Fabric scraps
Needle
Thread
Scissors

You can pick gourds fresh from a garden or find them in markets during the fall or winter.

To Make a Gourd Finger Puppet: Using the long, curved top of the gourd as the nose, paint on features for a face. Have an adult help you cut a hole in the bottom of the puppet's "head," and scoop out the contents with a spoon. Allow the gourd to dry, then use your finger as the puppet's neck.

To Make a Gourd Hand Puppet: Turn the gourd upside-down, and use the long, curved part as the neck. Paint a funny face on the "head." Sew clothes for your puppet from fabric scraps.

Now it's time for the show!

Traveling Shows

In the seventeenth century, hand puppets (figures with heads and a body of cloth that fit over the puppeteer's hand) became popular. They were easy to operate and did not cost a lot of money to make. Puppeteers would put on shows with puppet characters, such as Punch and Judy, from the backs of their wagons and on portable stages. Talk about taking the show on the road!

PASS IT ON!

Say what's on your mind, then pass it on!

WHAT YOU'LL NEED

Paper
Pen

With many parents working and kids participating in many after-school activities, one thing is for certain. Today's families are busy! Keep track of what's going on in your world—and in the worlds of your other family members—with this fun, "pass it on" weekly communication. Write a sentence about what you're doing or feeling, then pass it on to another family member. That member comments on your sentence and adds another. The note is again passed on to another family member, who comments on each of the previous comments and adds another of their own. Before you know it, the original letter comes back to you—and you have a quick idea of what everyone is doing and what each of your family members has to say.

SWITCH AND SHOW

One word can make all the difference.

WHAT YOU'LL NEED

Photocopies of a
popular story
Correction fluid for
copies
Markers
Paper

Have you ever stopped to think about how much difference just a few words can make? This fun game will answer that question with a grin. Pick your favorite short story, and photocopy it. On the photocopies, replace key words with similar but different words. If you picked *The Three Bears,* you could replace "three" with "fifteen," "bears" with "rabbits," and "porridge" with "celery." Don't forget to make the replacements everywhere that word is mentioned. Now read the story with the new words in place. Does it change the meaning of the story? The moral? Does it still make sense? Now illustrate your favorite moment in the updated story, just to remind you of the fun.

"TOUCHING" MAIL

Express how you feel, feel what you express.

Adult Help Needed

WHAT YOU'LL NEED

Scrap paper
Braille alphabet
Pencil
Card stock
Old nail polish
Markers

Feel the need to say hello? I love you? Goodbye? The next time you want to write what you feel, why not give your friends and family the chance to feel what you write?

Create your note using Braille. First, pick a simple message—1 to 3 words, tops. On a piece of scrap paper, translate the letters into the dot-patterned letters used by the visually impaired. (See the Braille chart on the next page for guidance.)

When you've translated your message, carefully copy it onto a clean piece of white card stock, leaving lots of space between letters and words. Drip small blobs of nail polish over the alphabet dots. This works best if the nail polish is old and slightly thickened. If you need to, go back over the dots with a second coat so the letters dry slightly raised. (Work in a well-ventilated room and away from any flames when you use nail polish.) On the back of the card, translate your message in ordinary letters.

Decorate the card, once it dries, and pass it on. This "hello" note will be remembered for a long time!

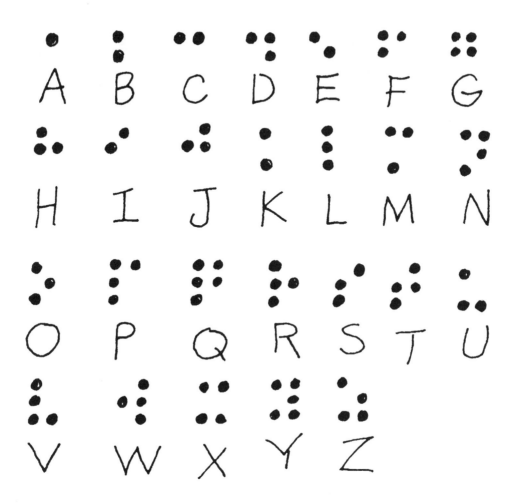

A GRANDPARENT'S STORY

When you combine your drawing with a grandparent's story, you create an intergenerational piece of artwork.

WHAT YOU'LL NEED

3×5-inch index cards
Pen
Envelope and stamps (optional)
Construction paper
Craft glue
Markers or colored pencils
Hole punch
Scissors
Yarn

Make a book about your grandparents. Think of some questions, and write each of them on an index card. Try to come up with at least 10 questions. You can ask, "What was your favorite toy?" or "Where did you live when you were 10 years old?" Have them write their answers on the cards. If your grandparents live far away, mail the cards to them and have them mail them back.

Once you have all the answers, glue each one to the bottom half of a sheet of construction paper. Draw a picture above the card to illustrate your grandparent's answer. Use markers or colored pencils to decorate a separate sheet of construction paper for the front cover of your book. To bind your book, set all the pages together and punch 4 holes along the left edge. Cut a piece of yarn, thread it through the holes, and tie it in a bow.

This book will become a family treasure!

What was your favorite toy?

A train

TV WORD TAG

This fast-paced channel-surfing game will keep your mind hopping!

WHAT YOU'LL NEED

Coin
TV and remote control
Timer
Paper
Pencils

Flip a coin to see who goes first in this fast-paced game. The first player holds the remote. Set the timer for 1 minute, and the first player has that amount of time to select a word heard on TV, shout it out, and write it on a piece of paper. Once that word is selected, the remote control is passed to the next player, who has 1 minute to flip through channels until he or she finds a word that rhymes with the first word. Once that word is discovered and called out, the remote goes to the next player, who must do the same.

TV tag continues until a player can't find a rhyming word. The player who can't find a rhyme gets a point. The player with the least points at the end of 20 minutes is the winner.

You can also play this game by trying to find synonyms rather than rhymes. A synonym is a word that means the same or almost the same as another. For example, "garbage," "trash," and "rubbish" are synonyms.

A TV Cat

In 1931, the Radio Corporation of America (RCA) broadcast experimental signals from the Empire State Building in New York City, featuring a familiar cartoon character, Felix the Cat. The first TV star was born!

FAMILY MATCH-UP

What's another word for sister? That depends on the sister.

If you've ever played memory match-up games—those face-down card games that dare you to find the 2 zebras for a match—this game gives a new twist to the age-old challenge. On a piece of scrap paper, make a list of the names of 10 family and friends: Mom, Dad, Sis, Cousin Bob, best friend Karen, etc. Then write down the 1 or 2 words that best describe each person. Funny? Computer wizard? Tall? Skier? Those descriptive words will represent the perfect match in this memory card game.

Write each name and each word on its own 3×3-inch piece of card stock. For each pair, mark a color-coded X so you'll know you've made the right match (for example, the card with "Dad" and the card that matches him, "Tall," will each have a purple X on them; the set for "Mom" and her match will each have a red X on them, etc.)

When you are finished making the game, mix up the cards and spread them all out, face down, on a flat surface. It's time to try your luck. Put all the pieces in a resealable plastic bag after you've finished playing your game. Lost pieces will make it hard to win (or play) the game!

FINGER PLAYS, FINGERS PLAY

Let your fingers do the talking.

WHAT YOU'LL NEED

Children's storybook
Paper
Pen
Copy machine
  (optional)
Highlighters
  (optional)
Cardboard box
Scissors
Paint and paintbrush
  (optional)
Washable glue
Washable markers
Fabric scraps
  (optional)
Video recorder
  (optional)

Is there a picture book you can't get enough of? A short children's story you never get tired of hearing? Why not put on a finger play based on that children's classic? Go through the story, and write out the main parts. For example, in *The Three Little Pigs,* the narrator, each pig, and the big bad wolf would be the main parts. You could also photocopy the pages of your favorite picture book and highlight each part in a different color—blue for the narrator; red, green, and yellow for the pigs; and purple for the big bad wolf.

Cut a stage out of a cardboard box, and decorate it if you'd like. Now it's time to get the actors ready! Use washable markers to decorate your fingers to look like the main characters. Draw pig faces on your middle, ring, and baby fingers. Add wolf ears to your index finger. Draw a big smile and bow tie for the narrator thumb. You can also make clothes out of fabric scraps. Act out the play for younger relatives or friends. You might want to ask a few teachers if you could perform this play in their classroom for the children. Have an adult videotape your play for an extra measure of fun. You'll giggle every time you watch it!

DINOSAUR FINGER PUPPET

Make a little thunder with a dinosaur on your hand!

WHAT YOU'LL NEED

Green paper
Scissors
Markers
Glue
Tape

MEDIUM

This unusual puppet's body is formed by your own hand. Paper cutouts make the long neck, the head, and the feet!

Cut out 2 identical head pieces. Cut out a neck piece that is 2 inches high and 2 inches wide. Decorate the head to look like your favorite dinosaur. Glue the tops of the 2 heads together. Roll the neck piece around your middle finger, and tape it. Slide the roll off your finger, and glue the bottom of the heads to the roll. For fun dino feet, cut 4 strips of paper that are 1 inch high and wide enough to wrap around your fingers.

Now it's time to dress the dinosaur! When the glue is dry on the head, slide your middle finger inside the neck piece. Tape the strips of paper around the tips of your other fingers.

Now you have a miniature dinosaur in, or should we say ON, your hands.

SELF-PORTRAITS

If a close friend or grandparent lives far away, make a self-portrait and mail it to them. It's better than a photograph!

WHAT YOU'LL NEED

Scissors
Grocery bags or brown mailing paper
Masking tape
Markers
Glue (optional)
Yarn and fabric scraps (optional)
Mailing tube

Cut up 2 or 3 grocery bags and tape them together end to end, or unroll a long sheet of mailing paper. Place the large sheet on the floor, and use masking tape to hold it down. Lie down on the paper, and have a friend or family member trace around your body. Decorate your outline with markers. If you want, glue on yarn for your hair and fabric scraps for your clothes. Make yourself into anything you want. You can be yourself, an astronaut, or a ballerina. Roll up the paper when the glue is completely dry, and, in a mailing tube, send it to someone special.

YARN STATIONERY

Make your letter writing a little more colorful.

WHAT YOU'LL NEED

Yarn scraps
Scissors
Craft glue
White paper

If you love to write letters but usually only have plain paper around, you're in luck. By using colorful scraps of yarn, you can brighten your day—and your letter! Cut little strips of yarn, and glue them to white paper to look like pretty flowers or floating balloons. Curve the yarn, around to create a cat or a bird. Fill your designs in with more yarn to make your stationery really bright, or create colorful outlines of shapes. The choice is up to you. Let your designs dry for at least 3 days before you write on the paper.

CUE CARD CRAZIES

Make your audience laugh with this fun-filled performance.

Is it time to put on a class or club program? Or are you and your friends in the mood to entertain your folks? Well, try this fun cue-card performance for a change of pace.

Pick a famous song or poem; "Row, Row, Row Your Boat" is a good example of what would work for this. Have everyone practice singing the song; playing a record or tape of the song would also work. Illustrate each word or key phrase of the song or poem on large, sturdy pieces of card stock or cardboard. Pass out the cards, and sing or play the song.

Each performer should flip up their word each time the word is said or sung. Practice until everyone gets it right. Now speed up the singing to see if the group can keep up. Before you know it, everyone will be giggling!

BOOKWORM BOOK BUDDY

Use this friendly stretch of a worm to keep track
of how many books you've read!

Cut out a 3-foot-long strip of construction paper; you may need to tape shorter pieces of paper together. On another piece of paper, draw and cut out a fun wormy head. Tape the head to the top of the body, and add worm markings along the body. Tape the worm to your wall (after getting your parents' permission!). Each time you finish reading a book, make a miniature book report. Write the title and the date you finished the book on the report, and tape it to your bookworm. Before you know it, your bookworm buddy will have a library on its back. And you'll have a great record of what you've read.

"WHO AM I" WORD COLLAGE

Even words can be art when self-expression is the goal.

When you think of the things you love, what words come to mind? Cooking? Dogs? Helping others? Painting? Now imagine—how can you bring those important words to life, using color? Choose a few of your favorite words, and write them on a large, sturdy piece of paper. (You may want to practice on scrap paper first, if you want to be extra neat.) Use lovely, unique lettering on your final collage, and decorate the letters with stripes and shapes. Use bold or pale colors to create the lettering, and you can surround the letters with tiny drawings and other descriptive words. It's your choice. Just experiment with colors and designs to make a single word or phrase paint a bigger picture. Share your artistically worded art with a friend or family member.

PERSONAL HEADLINES

Make a collage for friends and family to let them catch up on your life.

WHAT YOU'LL NEED

Old newspapers
Scissors
Card stock (cut in 4×6-inch pieces)
Glue
Markers
Postage stamps

Who are you? Where have you been? What are your hobbies? This fun fact-finding activity will help you express yourself—and share those expressions with the people who love you.

Go through a pile of old newspapers, cutting out and gathering words that express who you are, what you've done, and how you feel. Creatively position and glue those headlines on a side of a 4×6-inch piece of card stock. Make sure you glue all the edges down securely so they can't be ripped off. Decorate those words with colorful markers, if you like. Once the glue and ink are dry (plan for overnight drying time in most climates), add a stamp, an address, a quick "hello" to the back of the card, and drop it in a mailbox.

Your personal headlines will bring your friends and family up to date on your life.

OWL BOOKMARK

Whooooo's whooooo? This bookmark can help you keep track.

MEDIUM

WHAT YOU'LL NEED
Construction paper
Scissors
Craft glue
Clothespin

Keep track of whooooo's whooooo with this know-it-all bookmark. Cut out a triangle of brown paper for the top of the owl's head and a smaller yellow triangle for the beak. Cut large circles of white paper and smaller circles of black paper for eyes. Glue all the pieces onto the large brown triangle, and then glue the brown triangle onto the clothespin. Once the glue dries, use your owl to remind you what page ended your last reading adventure and what page will begin your next. Once you get the hang of making the owl, create other bookmarks using other animals or subjects. It'll be a great way to leave your own personal "mark."

WACKY WORD SEARCH

Can you find yourself in the mix?

MEDIUM

WHAT YOU'LL NEED
Paper
Pens
Copy machine

Have you ever done a word-search puzzle? Found the names of your favorite animals or rock bands or cartoon characters mixed in a sea of random letters? This is your chance to make a word search of your own starring—who else—YOU! First make a list of words that sum up who you are and what you like. Include your first, last, and middle name, of course. Then think about what things make you unique. Do you speak Spanish? Put "Spanish" on the list. Do you collect glass horses? Include the word "horses" in your search. Do you jump rope for fun? Don't forget to include "jump rope." Now mix those words, up and down, side to side, backward, and diagonally, in an ocean of unrelated letters. Make a few copies of your puzzle. Then see how long it takes your mom, dad, and best friend to find all the words. Or wait a few days, and test yourself!

FELT STORYBOARDS

Turn a pizza box into a storyboard, and bring the story to life with felt pictures.

WHAT YOU'LL NEED

Unused medium-size pizza box
Felt in assorted colors
Scissors
Craft glue
Markers
Trims (chenille stems, straw, yarn, plastic bags, etc.)

To make the storyboard background, cut 2 pieces of dark-colored felt to fit the inside of the top and bottom of the pizza box. Apply a layer of glue to the inside top and bottom of the box. Place both felt background pieces in the box over the glue. Let the glue dry completely.

Using assorted colors of felt, cut out felt pieces to make a picture. For example, if you were telling the story of *The Three Little Pigs,* you would need 3 pig cutouts, 1 wolf cutout, and 3 house cutouts. Draw features on the pieces with markers. Draw the eyes, noses, and mouths on the pigs. Glue a small piece of curled chenille stem for the tail, and glue on cutout felt overalls. Draw in the eyes, nose, mouth, and teeth on the wolf. Decorate each house with markers, felt, and other trims. Glue or draw straw on one house, some twigs on another, and red felt bricks to the last house. Place your pieces on the felt background to tell your story.

REBUS STORY

The next time friends come to play, ask everyone to make a rebus story. Then they can give their story to someone else to tell.

WHAT YOU'LL NEED
Black felt-tip pen
Drawing paper
Markers
Construction paper
Paper punch
Scissors
Yarn

Create a story with pictures for words. You can make up your own story or use your favorite fairy tale. Write your story on a piece of paper. As you write it down, draw certain words, especially repeated words, as a picture. For example, if you wrote a story about a king, you could draw a picture of a crown as the symbol for the word "king." Write and draw a whole story, then bind the pieces of paper together to make a book.

Binding instructions: To make the front and back cover, fold a sheet of construction paper in half and punch 4 holes near the fold. Decorate the front page. Then punch 4 holes in each of the finished pages, making sure they line up with the holes on the cover. Place the pages inside the cover. Cut a piece of yarn, thread it though the holes, and tie it in a bow.

Once upon a 🕐, the 👑 visited the 🏰.

It was the 👑's birthday. He ate .

MOVIE-TIME SCRAPBOOK

You become the film critic!

WHAT YOU'LL NEED
Spiral notebook
Craft supplies (construction paper, ribbon, sequins, etc.)
Craft glue
Movie ads
Scissors
Ticket stubs
Pens

Are you a film buff? Does going to the latest movie totally rev your jets? Then this fun project is custom-made for you. Keep a movie scrapbook!

Decorate the cover of a spiral notebook any way you'd like—be creative. Dedicate each page of the notebook to a movie you want to see. Headed for the latest Leonardo DiCaprio flick? Check magazines and newspapers for print advertisements or reviews of that film. Cut them out, and glue them to the page. Once you actually see the film, date the page, glue on your ticket stub, and take a minute to jot down whether or not the movie was all you'd hoped it would be.

Years from now you'll look back on the scrapbook as a sign of the times. When you're older, you can see how your taste in movies has changed or stayed the same.

Galloping Into the Movies

Would you believe that movies got their start because of a horse? A row of cameras was lined up to take pictures of a moving horse. When the horse galloped by, each camera got a slightly different picture. Showing the still pictures quickly created a film by tricking the viewer's eyes into seeing motion!

STORY TIME TWIST

Cutting up has never been more fun.

MEDIUM

WHAT YOU'LL NEED
Scrap paper
Tape
Pens
4 jars or cans
Tape recorder
(optional)

Storytelling is a tradition almost as old as humankind itself. Add a crazy new twist to this ancient art with a few scraps of paper and your imagination.

Gather 2 or more friends together. Ask each friend to come up with 4 nouns (a person, place, or thing), 4 verbs (action words—like sing, run, fly), 4 adjectives (words that describe nouns—like round, slippery, blue), and 4 adverbs (words that describe verbs—like quickly, brightly, differently). Have them write each word on an individual scrap of paper.

While your friends are doing this, make a label with paper and tape for each jar. Mark the labels "nouns," "verbs," "adjectives," "adverbs." Then your friends should drop their words in the appropriate jar.

To begin the storytelling, each person should draw 1 paper from each jar. The first person begins a story, based on the 4 words they drew. The second adds to the story, using their words, and so on. Record the crazy work of fiction, and play it back later for extra fun. If you don't have a tape recorder, write the story down to share with others.

STEP IN, STEP OUT

When you write the sequel, you can become your favorite hero!

MEDIUM

WHAT YOU'LL NEED
Favorite novel
Paper
Pen

Do you have an all-time-favorite book? An all-time-favorite book character? If you do, and you've ever wondered what happened after the story's final page, this is your chance to take control.

Become your favorite hero or heroine when you write the sequel. Ask yourself a few important questions: How did the events in your favorite story affect and change the character? How did it affect the characters around him or her? And most important, what might have happened next in your favorite character's life? Write it out in a short story follow-up. For more fun, invite a few friends over to act out your new story. Write speaking parts for everyone, rehearse, and then put on a show!

STATIONERY SET

Use these cards to write thank-you letters or to just say "hi" to faraway friends.

MEDIUM

WHAT YOU'LL NEED
Envelopes
Scissors
Construction paper
Ruled writing paper
Craft glue
Markers

To make your own stationery, you can use plain envelopes or make your own. To make the notecards, cut and fold over a piece of construction paper, making sure it will fit inside the envelope. Unfold the construction-paper notecard. Cut a piece of writing paper to fit inside the notecard, and glue it in place. Repeat this procedure to make a set of notecards. Use markers to decorate each notecard. Draw a simple design, such as a series of stripes, curvy lines, or polka dots. Or cut a rippled edge at the bottom of each notecard so a bit of the writing paper shows. This gives the card a lacy look. Draw a matching design on the envelopes, leaving room for the stamp, the address, and your return address.

NET SCAPE

Use the Internet to express your artful side.

MEDIUM

WHAT YOU'LL NEED

Computer with Internet access
Printer
Blank paper
White glue
Pen

Are you in full command of the World Wide Web and eager to make that connection clear? Why not surf the 'Net for a few cyber sensations, and turn those discoveries into art?

Go to your favorite Internet search engine. Type in a fun topic (a name, a band you like, a country in Asia, a flavor of ice cream), and see what comes into view. If you find a picture, statement, or logo that really makes you smile, print it out and set it aside. Once you get 4 or 5 great printouts, turn them into an expressive cyber collage. Be sure to date the back of the page and put it in a safe place. Pull it out in weeks or years to enjoy it all over again.

AUTHOR! AUTHOR!

Tell your favorite author just what his or her words mean to you.

EASY

WHAT YOU'LL NEED

Stationery or lined paper
Pen
Envelope
Stamp
Computer with Internet access (optional)

Is there an author who writes books that you can't put down? Why not drop your favorite author a line to tell them exactly what their books have meant to you? You can write to the company that published the books—the address will be inside your book. Keep your letter neat and brief, but don't hesitate to tell the writer exactly how you feel. Did the book make you happy? Sad? Thoughtful? Mad? Tell the author. And if you decided to try writing a sequel to one of their books (as in Step In, Step Out on page 196), send that along with your note. If you have a computer, you can try looking up the author's name on an Internet search engine.

Your favorite author will be pleased and flattered and might even write you back!

PICTURE PERFECT PROGRESS

Who are you? How have you changed?

WHAT YOU'LL NEED

Old photos
Copy machine
   (optional)
White glue
Blank paper
Pen

Most people have wondered what they'll look like when they grow up, grow older, and even grow old. If you've ever had those thoughts, this activity is just for you.

Ask your parents for a box or scrapbook of old photographs of yourself. Then ask if there are a few copies you can keep for yourself. (You can make photocopies of the pictures—this works just as well.) Select photos that show how you've changed...and how you've stayed the same. Want some examples? How about the picture taken at the hospital on the day you headed home after being born? How about a photo showing your first tooth? A picture that shows how you got that cute little scar on your left cheek? How about one that shows how your dark hair used to be light?

Arrange those telling photographs on a blank page of paper, and write a caption under each shot. Ask your parents for help if you're not totally clear on the details. Now study those photos. Close your eyes, and look to the future. You might get a better idea of just what's to come.

Now draw a picture of what you envision you'll look like in the coming years. Keep this portrait someplace safe so you can look at it later to see how accurate you were!

HOLIDAY IDEAS

Scientists probe the questions of how things work and why they act the way they do. But science is not just for scientists. Everyone is interested in the world around them and what makes things tick. You can learn a great deal about your world by observing and performing experiments right in your own backyard or kitchen. Here are some activities to get you started investigating at home!

STAR OF DAVID BOOKMARKS

Latkes are not the only use you'll have for potatoes this Hanukkah!

MEDIUM

Adult Help Needed

WHAT YOU'LL NEED

Firm, raw potatoes
Knife
Paper towels
Marker
Construction paper
Paintbrush
Paints
Scissors
Hole punch
Ribbon

Have an adult help you with the cutting in this project. Choose and wash a firm potato. Cut it in half. Pat the potato dry with a paper towel. Using a marker, draw a Star of David on the white part of the potato half. Carefully cut away the potato around the star outline. When you finish, you will have a raised star.

Cut 12-inch-long rectangles from construction paper to make the bookmarks—cut them a little wider than your potato star shape. Brush a thick, even layer of paint onto the star shape. Carefully press it onto the bookmark where you want a star. Lift the potato straight up—don't wiggle or drag it when you lift it. Print a row of stars along the bookmark. Try painting half the potato shape with a color and the other half a different color!

When the paint has dried, write messages on the bookmarks, such as "Happy Hanukkah" or the person's name you are giving the bookmark to. Punch a hole in the top of the bookmark, and thread the ribbon through the hole. These Hanukkah gifts can be enjoyed all year long!

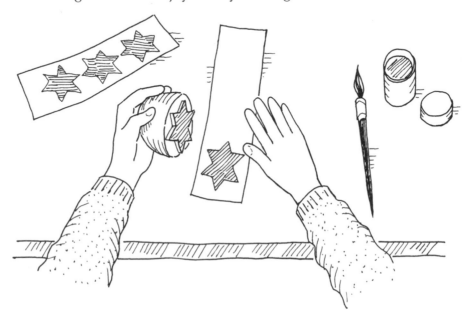

HANUKKAH SPINNING STARS

Watch the stars spin on this colorful mobile!

WHAT YOU'LL NEED

8¹/₂×11-inch white paper
Pencil
Scissors
Colored construction paper
String
Craft glue or tape

Fold the piece of white paper in half. Draw ½ of a large Star of David on the paper, keeping the center of the star on the folded edge of the paper. Unfold the paper, and draw 2 more stars inside the larger star. Cut out the stars, trimming each so it's a little smaller than the next—but be sure you keep the Star of David shape.

Place the open star patterns on a piece of colored construction paper, and trace around them. Cut out each star. You should have 3 stars: 1 large, 1 medium, 1 small. Line up the stars, 1 inside the next.

Cut 2 pieces of string; the strings should be slightly longer than the distance between the inside star and the next bigger star. Glue or tape the string in place, but be sure the smaller stars move inside the larger stars. Cut another, longer piece of string, and glue or tape the string to the top of the largest star. Make a loop at the end of the top string for hanging.

Hang the mobile away from a wall, then watch the stars spin. (Note: Try shiny wrapping paper for shimmery, shiny stars.)

HANUKKAH CANDLE CUTOUTS

Make these shimmering candle cutouts to put in your window or doorway—one for each day of Hanukkah.

DIFFICULT

Adult Help Needed

WHAT YOU'LL NEED

Cardboard
Pencil
Craft knife (adult use only)
Black construction paper
Scissors
Colored cellophane or tissue paper
Tape
Newspaper
Old crayons (yellow, red, orange)
Cheese grater
Waxed paper
Iron
Craft glue
Hole punch
String or yarn

These are instructions for making 1 candle—but make as many as you'd like to hang. On a rectangle of cardboard, draw a candle shape and a flame shape (see the illustration below). Ask an adult to cut out the shapes using the craft knife; this is your tracing stencil. Make 2 equal-size rectangles from black paper. Use the cardboard to trace the candle and flame shapes onto the black rectangles. Cut out the shapes. Pick a color of cellophane or tissue paper, and cut a rectangle slightly larger than the candle stem. Tape the colored paper to a black rectangle so it covers the cutout stem shape.

Cover your work surface with old newspaper. Carefully grate the crayons to get shavings. Cut two 4-inch squares of waxed paper, and place the shavings on a waxed-paper square. Place the other square on top of the first. Now cover the crayon shavings with more newspaper. Have an adult use an iron (on the dry setting) to press lightly on the newspaper.

When the waxed paper is cool, cut out a piece slightly larger than the candle-flame shape. Tape or glue the waxed paper creation to the black paper so it shines through. To finish, glue the second sheet of black paper to the back of the first. Punch a hole in the top, thread with string or yarn, and hang.

EDIBLE MENORAHS

These menorahs look great and are yummy to eat!

WHAT YOU'LL NEED

Bread
Cream cheese or butter
Butter knife
Pretzel sticks
Carrot stick
Raisins

Spread bread with cream cheese or butter, and arrange 8 pretzels on the bread as candles. Poke them through the bread so they stand up. Use the carrot stick as the shammes, the candle that is used to light the other candles. Put the carrot stick behind the other candles. Place raisins as flames at the ends of the carrot and pretzel sticks—you may need to use a dot of cream cheese to make them stay. Use this menorah as a centerpiece for your seder.

Light the Way

During the festival of Hanukkah, menorahs are lit for eight days. So why are there nine candles on the menorah? There is a candle for each night of the holiday, and the other candle is called the shammes, or servant. This candle is used to light all the others.

CHRISTMAS CARD PANORAMA

Use old Christmas cards to make a festive scene in a box!

WHAT YOU'LL NEED

Shoe box
Construction paper
Glue
Scissors
Crayons
Old Christmas cards

Decorate the shoe box by gluing squares of construction paper onto the sides and drawing and gluing shapes onto that. Cut out pictures from Christmas cards to make a scene inside the box. It can be a realistic setting with trees and stars or a fantastic scene where toys float through the sky and a tiny Santa looks up at a giant child. Use your imagination!

For a 3-dimensional panoramic scene, cut out a tab on the bottom of some pictures to make them stand. Save this year's cards to make a new panorama next year. Make one each year, and stack them together to make a really spectacular Christmas display!

A Christmas Tan?

In Australia, the festive scenes at Christmas don't include any snowmen. In fact, Christmas in Australia is never white. That's because Christmas in Australia takes place during the summer! Lots of families enjoy their holiday dinner at the park or on the beach.

STRAW STAR

Weave straws together for a glittering treat.

MEDIUM

WHAT YOU'LL NEED

2 plastic drinking straws
Scissors
String or yarn
Craft glue
Glitter

Who knew ordinary drinking straws could become glittering holiday stars? It's true—they can be works of art. Cut the straws in half; be sure the halves are even. Take a long piece of string or yarn in your hand, at least 18 inches long. Criss-cross 4 straw halves so they are in a star pattern, then wrap the string around the middle of the pieces, being careful to keep the string tight in the center. Weave around the straws at the middle, pulling the straws slightly apart as you weave to keep the arms of the star separated. Once you've made the weave secure, knot the string, leaving a little dangling as a hanger. Spread glue on the straw star, and sprinkle it with glitter. Now make enough stars to decorate your house for the holidays!

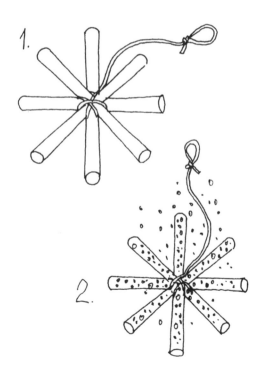

CANDY CANE REINDEER

Rudolph never tasted so good!

WHAT YOU'LL NEED
Candy cane
Brown chenille stem
2 wiggle eyes
Craft glue
Small red pom-pom

This candy ornament is as fun to eat as it is to make. But don't eat it too quickly. You'll want to enjoy seeing it on your Christmas tree. Take an unbroken candy cane, still wrapped in plastic wrap, and twist a brown chenille stem around the curve so the 2 ends are even. Twist the chenille stem so it is secured to Rudolph's head—we don't want Rudolph's antlers to slip! Bend the ends of the chenille stems to create the reindeer's antlers. Glue a wiggle eye on either side of the slope of the curve of the candy cane. Add a red pom-pom nose to the end of the curve, and spruce up your Christmas tree with your candy cane reindeer!

SILVER BELL ORNAMENTS

Make your own jingle bells to hang from the Christmas tree.

EASY

WHAT YOU'LL NEED

Cardboard egg
   carton
Scissors
Colored string
Wooden beads
Needle
Silver paint
Paintbrush
Ribbon

These bells may not make music, but they will help make your holidays a singing success!

Cut a single egg carton cup for each bell. String a bead on a string, and secure it with a knot. Ask an adult to help you use a needle to poke the free end of the string through the egg carton cup. Make a knot in the string on the inside of the egg carton, making sure the bead swings freely inside the egg cup.

When you have made 3 bells, tie them to a longer string. Paint the bells silver. Tie a ribbon in a bow around the long string. Hang the ornament on your Christmas tree, and gather the family around to sing "Jingle Bells."

Do I Have the Wrong Title?

You may think of "Jingle Bells" as a Christmas song, but did you know that it was first performed for a Thanksgiving program at composer James Pierpont's church? The words and music were written in 1857, and the original song title wasn't "Jingle Bells." The song was called "One Horse Open Sleigh."

KWANZA BAG

This beautiful bag is a great gift—full or empty!

MEDIUM

WHAT YOU'LL NEED

Burlap
Scissors
Measuring tape
Embroidery thread
Needle
Ribbon or cord
Safety pin
Marker

Cut a piece of burlap 10×14 inches. Along the 14-inch side, fold the burlap down an inch to make a tube. Sew the bottom of this tube closed, leaving the sides open so you can thread a ribbon or cord through it for the bag's drawstring.

Tie the ribbon or cord to a safety pin, and thread it through the tube. Remove the safety pin, and make a knot in both ends of the cord. Use a marker to write the word "Kwanza" on the bag's front. Draw some decorative shapes or lines around the word if you wish. Use embroidery thread in the traditional African colors of red, green, and black to sew along the word Kwanza and whatever else you have drawn.

Then fold the bag in half so that the drawstring is at the top and the design is on the inside. Stitch the sides of the bag together, and turn the bag right side out. You can give the empty bag as a gift, or fill it with small toys or Kwanza treats.

A Language for All of Africa

Fill your Kwanza bag with fruit since Kwanza means "first fruits" in Swahili, a language spoken in much of Africa. Swahili words were chosen for Kwanza so that African Americans would remember that all of Africa is their ancestral home, not just one country.

KWANZA PARTY FAVORS

Make a miniature flag favor for each person you invite to your karamu, or Kwanza, celebration feast.

WHAT YOU'LL NEED

White construction paper
Scissors
Red, black, and green markers
Craft glue
Toothpicks

Cut small rectangles (about 1½×1 inches) from white paper. Color the top third of each rectangle red, the middle third black, and the bottom third green. Glue each of these flags to a toothpick pole by dabbing glue on the back edge of each square. Then roll the glued edge around a toothpick.

Stick the decorated toothpick in a cupcake or other food to make the flag stand up—and the goodies stand out!

What's the News?

Kwanza is celebrated for seven days, with a special principle or belief, such as Unity, celebrated on each day. Many people start the nightly celebrations by asking, "Habari Gani?" That means, "What's the news?" To respond, they answer with the word for the principle of the day.

KWANZA CANDLE SURPRISE

These "pretend" candles in red, green, and black are filled with surprises! They make perfect party favors for your Kwanza celebration.

Adult Help Needed

WHAT YOU'LL NEED

Paper towel tubes (1 tube will make 2 candles)

Scissors

Craft glue

Black, red, and green construc- tion paper

Orange or yellow tissue paper

Ruler

Individually wrapped candy

Nuts in the shell

Small prizes

Cut each tube in half (ask an adult for help with the cutting). Then glue a piece of black, green, or red construction paper to each tube.

Cut a 10-inch square of tissue paper, and place candy, nuts, and a small prize in the middle of the square. Gather the tissue paper up around the prize, and push the wrapped candy and prize into the tube so the ends of the tissue stick out like a candle flame.

For party favors, make 1 for each person at your table. You could also write each person's name on a candle and use them for name cards for dinner!

BIRCH BARK VALENTINES

*Make special valentines out of natural treasures
and your own verse.*

WHAT YOU'LL NEED

Thin birch bark (use only fallen or loose bark that is peeling off naturally)
Collected natural objects (flowers, rocks, twigs, leaves, etc.)
Ink pen
Ribbon

The paper birch is an unusual and delicate tree. Its waterproof white bark was used by Native Americans to make canoes. It can also be used like paper to make these valentines.

Find a paper birch tree with thin strips of bark that have fallen or are already peeling off. Tear off only what you will use. Be careful not to tear off living bark—it could harm the tree!

Next, take a walk in a park, woodland, or other place where you can find early flowers, feathers, or evergreen twigs. With permission, collect a few natural treasures that you think are pretty. Lay your treasures out at home, and let them inspire a valentine poem. Evergreen twigs may make you think of a friendship that is "ever green." Flowers may stand for a blossoming friendship.

When you have composed your poem, write it on the piece of birch bark. Roll the bark around the feathers, flowers, or whatever objects you have used in your verse. Tie the valentine with a ribbon, and surprise someone on Valentine's Day—or any day!

VALENTINE IDEAS

Valentine's Day is a time to say you care about others.
Show them how much with these heartfelt ideas.

WHAT YOU'LL NEED

Doilies
Scissors
Red and white con-
     struction paper
Craft glue
Glitter
Satin ribbon
Craft stick
Plastic sandwich bag
     (optional)
Valentine candy
     (optional)

Doily Cards: Cut heart shapes from doilies, and glue them on red and white construction paper hearts. Use glue to write "Be Mine" on the doily. Cover the glue with glitter. Tie satin ribbon in small bows, and glue them on the doily cards. Once the glue has dried, shake off the excess glitter.

Heart & Arrow Cards: Cut a heart shape from red construction paper. Cut a smaller heart from white construction paper, and glue it on top of the red heart. Make an arrow from a craft stick and construction paper; glue the paper to the craft stick. Glue the arrow to the hearts. Write a valentine message for someone special.

If you want, attach a plastic sandwich bag filled with valentine candy to let your valentine know just how sweet he or she is!

Be Mine

VALENTINE HOLDER

Make a valentine holder that looks like a miniature castle.

Cover your work surface with newspaper. Arrange your box or boxes how you would like them to be. Cut the paper towel tubes to different lengths, and arrange them on your boxes. For a castle, use a large tissue box for the main building, then put paper towel rolls on the ends for turrets. When you are happy with the arrangement, it's time to decorate your architecture!

Glue construction paper to cover the box(es) and the paper towel tubes. Replace your box(es) and paper towel tubes, and glue them together. Cut a slit in the top of the main box to place your Valentine's Day cards. Decorate your building with paint, glitter, stickers, ribbon—whatever you want!

VALENTINE'S DAY HEART WREATH

Cover a paper plate with cut-out hearts in various sizes and colors (maybe reds and pinks) for a terrific Valentine's Day decoration!

WHAT YOU'LL NEED

Construction paper
Scissors
Ruler
Paper plate
Craft glue
Yarn or ribbon

From the construction paper, cut out hearts in several different sizes (½ inch, 1 inch, 1½ inches, and 2 inches would be good sizes). You can choose a color theme (pink and white hearts), or you can make a multicolored heart wreath. You'll want to cut out a lot of hearts.

Cut the middle out of a paper plate, and throw the middle away. Glue the hearts over the remaining plate to make a valentine wreath. Make small bows with yarn or ribbon, and glue them to the wreath. Make a loop out of yarn or ribbon, and glue it on the back to hang your wreath.

VALENTINE'S DAY PINS

*These heart-shaped pins are simple to make. Once you wear one,
everyone will want one of their own!*

Adult Help Needed

WHAT YOU'LL NEED

Dough (1 cup flour, 1
cup warm water,
2 teaspoons
cream of tartar,
1 teaspoon oil,
1/4 cup salt, food
coloring)
Measuring cup
Mixing bowl
Mixing spoon
Medium saucepan
Pot holder
Waxed paper
Heart-shaped cookie
cutter
1/4 cup flour
Cotton swabs
(optional)
Pin backs
Craft glue
Paint and paintbrush
(optional)
Clear varnish
(optional)

Mix all the dough ingredients, adding the food coloring last. Ask an adult to help you stir this over medium heat on the stove until smooth. Remove the mixture from the pan, and knead it until it is well blended. (Have an adult check to make sure the dough is cool enough to handle!)

To make the valentine pins, use your hands to work the dough on waxed paper until the dough is about ¼ inch thick. Dip the cookie cutter in flour to prevent the dough from sticking, and cut out a heart. If you'd like to personalize the pins, stick the end of a cotton swab in food coloring and write a name. You can also add other decorations to the pin.

Press the pin back into the heart while the dough is still damp. Allow the pin to dry for a day. (Add a few drops of glue if the pin back isn't stuck well in the dough.) You can paint or apply clear varnish to your heart after it is thoroughly dry.

LEPRECHAUN BUBBLE PIPE

Legend says that fairies catch rides on bubbles
made from leprechaun pipes!

MEDIUM

Adult Help Needed

WHAT YOU'LL
NEED

Acorn
Kitchen knife
Nail
Straw
Cool-temp glue gun
    and glue
1 cup warm water
½ cup green dish-
    washing liquid
1 teaspoon salt
Bowl
Plastic spoon

Find a large acorn. With adult help, cut the top off and dig out the meat to make a little bowl. Using the nail, carefully make a hole in the side near the bottom of the bowl, just big enough for the straw to fit through. Using the cool-temp glue gun (with adult help), put the straw into the hole and fill the area around the straw with glue. Blow gently through the straw to make sure no glue is clogging the hole. Set the bubble pipe aside.

Mix up some bubble solution by mixing 1 cup warm water, ½ cup green dish-washing liquid, and 1 teaspoon salt together in a bowl. Stir until the salt dissolves.

Now it's time to give some rides to some leprechauns! Dip the pipe in the bubble solution, and blow gently.

CHENILLE STEM PALS

Make some little people even the Irish would love.

WHAT YOU'LL NEED

Green chenille stems
Scissors
Green paper
Markers
Cotton balls
Craft glue
Small safety pin
(optional)

Make your own band of lively leprechauns out of chenille stems, paper, and imagination.

Bend a green chenille stem in half. Cut out a paper circle, draw a face on it, and add a cottony wisp of a white beard. Cut out and glue a hat to the top of his head. Twist a second chenille stem around the body to make wee arms. If you'd like to make a pin out of your friend, glue the back (the side that doesn't open) of a small safety pin to the back of the leprechaun's head.

Now you've got a green friend you can carry or wear to inspire a smile. You'll be in the green as long as your little friend is near. Make other people when you finish your leprechaun. Use your imagination, and come up with your own fun guys and gals!

SPRING PLACE MATS

These make great gifts for grandparents and people in nursing homes, or use them yourself at mealtime.

MEDIUM

Adult Help Needed

WHAT YOU'LL NEED

Dried, pressed spring flowers, including stems and leaves

Clear vinyl adhesive paper

Yardstick

Scissors

If you can't find dried flowers at your local craft store, dry your own! Place spring flowers between 2 pieces of white paper, and put the paper inside the pages of a thick book for a few weeks. When the flowers are completely dried, use them for this project.

For each place mat, measure and cut 2 pieces of clear vinyl adhesive paper into rectangles that are approximately 12×18 inches. Peel the backing off 1 piece of paper, and lay it sticky side up on the table. Place the dried flowers on the sticky side of the paper. Press everything flat with your fingers. Some flowers will work better if you remove the petals and use the petals individually.

Peel the backing off the second piece of adhesive paper. Carefully place it sticky side down over your arrangement. Don't worry about lining up the edges exactly. (TIP: Have an adult help with the contact paper. You can each hold 2 corners, and it will be easier to place without causing wrinkles.) Press everything down as flat as possible, and your place mat will look beautiful. Trim the edges with scissors.

CRACKED PICTURES

Make beautiful mosaics from Easter eggshells!

MEDIUM

WHAT YOU'LL NEED

Leftover Easter eggshells
Colored markers
Construction paper
Craft glue

Wash and dry the shell bits. Collect an assortment of shapes and sizes. A lot of the shells will still have their color, but if you use plain eggshells, color them with markers. Draw the simple outline of an animal, person, or some favorite object on a piece of construction paper. You might want to use a dark piece of paper to contrast with your shells. Glue the shells into the outline. Glue them close together so no paper shows through. When you have filled in the outline completely, let the glue dry. Color in the details with markers.

MINI-EASTER BASKETS

These are so simple, you'll want to make plenty to use as table decorations and to give to your friends.

EASY

Adult Help Needed

WHAT YOU'LL NEED

Cardboard egg cartons
Scissors
Pencil
Ribbon or chenille stems
Paints and paintbrushes (optional)
Easter grass (or shredded green construction paper)
Easter candy

Separate the individual egg buckets of an egg carton with scissors; an adult may need to help you do this. Use a sharp pencil point to poke a hole on 2 opposite sides of each bucket. Cut a piece of ribbon, and tie each end through a hole to create a handle for the basket. Instead of ribbon, you could use chenille stems for the handle; attach each end of the stem to a side of the basket. Add a bow to the top of the handle. Paint the baskets, if you'd like. Fill the basket with Easter grass and Easter goodies.

FUNNY BUNNY

Turn a baby food jar into a "Funny Bunny" with this fun craft idea!

WHAT YOU'LL NEED

Baby food jar
Cotton balls
Construction paper
Scissors
Markers (optional)
Glue

Fill a baby food jar with cotton balls. Cut out a large heart that is a little taller and wider than the front of the jar. You can draw a face on this heart, if you'd like. Cut out a medium heart that is about 1 inch larger than the base of the jar. Cut out 2 small hearts that are about the size of a penny. Glue the large heart to the front of the jar. The top of the heart should extend beyond the top of the jar and look like ears. Glue the medium heart to the base of the jar so the top of the heart extends beyond the front of the jar. The top of the heart that sticks out from the base will look like feet. Glue small hearts on the sides of the jar for hands. Glue a cotton ball to the back of the jar for a tail.

A Dough Bunny?

The bunny first became an Easter symbol in Germany in the 1500s, but it was another 300 years before the first edible Easter bunnies were made. But these first edible bunnies weren't made of chocolate; they were made of pastry and sugar!

BUNNY EASTER BASKET

This cute basket looks just like the Easter Bunny!

WHAT YOU'LL NEED

1 pint milk carton
Scissors
White and pink
   cotton balls
Craft glue
Construction paper
Easter grass
Easter goodies

Open the spout of an empty, clean pint milk carton. Lay the carton on a table with the spout side on the table. Cut out the side that is now on the top of the carton. You now have a rectangular hole. Glue white cotton balls all over the remaining milk carton; be sure to cover it completely. The opened spout of the milk carton is the nose of the rabbit. Place a pink cotton ball on the spout for the nose and add a pink one in the back for a tail. Cut out 2 paper eyes, and glue them just above the spout. Cut out 2 long ears, and glue them on either side of the carton—your rabbit can be a flop-eared bunny with ears that hang down or the ears can stand up. Place Easter grass in the hole, and fill the bunny with goodies.

RIBBON SPOOL SACHET

This present will look pretty and smell great—what
more could Mom want?

**WHAT YOU'LL
NEED**
Large ribbon spool
Tissue paper
Baby powder
Ribbon

Ever wondered what you could do with those big, plastic ribbon spools once you've used up the ribbon? Check out this fun, frilly sachet.

Take 2 pieces of lovely tissue paper, and spread them out on a flat surface. Place the spool in the center. Sprinkle a good amount of baby power inside the circular spool. Draw the tissue paper up around the spool to form a pretty puff. Tie the top of the tissue paper with colorful ribbon. When you give this to Mom it will remind her that you think no one is quite as sweet as she.

LOVED ONE LOCKET

Be close to Mom all year long when she wears your photograph inside a pretty locket.

WHAT YOU'LL NEED
2 twist-off bottle caps
Colored nail polish
Felt scraps
Scissors
Craft glue
Small photo of your face
Silk cord

Locket necklaces are a wonderful way to hold photographs of loved ones. Your mother will be especially happy to receive this one—after all, it has your face inside and you made it yourself!

Paint both bottle caps inside and out with a light coat of colored nail polish. Paint a side at a time, use even strokes, and let dry for at least 15 minutes before continuing. You may need to add a second coat to cover the bottle cap well.

Cut a small strip of felt in a color that matches the nail polish. Glue an end inside each cap to form a hinge. This will allow the caps to close and form a locket. Cut out and glue another piece of felt inside a cap, and glue a picture of your face, also cut to fit, inside the other cap. Cut out a small heart, and glue it inside the first cap.

Make sure the felt hinge is at the top of the locket and your photo is face-up when the cap hangs. You might want to cut out a small felt heart or other decoration to glue to the outside of the locket. When the glue has dried, tie a silk cord around the hinge of the locket. Then tie the ends together to form a loop large enough to fit over an adult head.

Whenever Mom wears her locket, you'll be close to her heart!

Mom Gets Her Day

The origins of Mother's Day began in ancient Greece to honor Rhea, mother earth. It wasn't until 1914 that President Woodrow Wilson declared an official day to honor moms. Ana Jarvis started her campaign in 1907 to get moms their special day!

MOM AND ME BOOK

This book is sure to bring tears of joy to Mom's eyes!

WHAT YOU'LL NEED

25 small brown paper bags
Scissors
Two 9-inch squares heavy cardboard
Iron
Pencil
Metal ruler
Clear plastic tape
Wrapping paper
Craft glue
Hole punch
2 clothespins
Ribbon
Markers

Along a seam, cut a side of a brown bag to the bottom. Cut the bottom off the bag. Repeat for all the bags. Unfold the bags. Trim the bags to the size of the cardboard (9-inch squares). Have an adult help you iron the bags with a cool iron to make them lay flat.

Draw a line 1 inch from an edge of each of the cardboard squares. Use the edge of the ruler to bend the cardboard along the line. Bend the cardboard back and forth, until it works like a paper hinge. Put a strip of plastic tape on each side of the cardboard covering the hinge. Glue wrapping paper on the cardboard.

Punch holes in the 1-inch section of the covers; punch a hole 2 inches from the top of the book and another hole 2 inches from the bottom. Punch holes in the paper bag pages to match the cover holes. Stack all the bags between the covers, and clamp them with the clothespins.

Thread the ribbon from the inside to the outside of the cover. Tie the ribbon in a knot, and make a bow. Write a title on the front cover, and decorate it. Fill your book with thoughts and pictures of Mom.

HEARTS AND FLOWERS BOOKMARK

Give Mom your heart—and the time to enjoy a good book.

WHAT YOU'LL NEED
Construction paper
Scissors
Clear vinyl adhesive paper
Colorful cord
Paper clip

Make this fun and easy bookmark—and promise her you'll keep yourself and your siblings busy for at least 15 minutes a day so she can quietly read and put your creation to use.

Cut 3 hearts and 3 flower shapes out of different colored construction paper. Play with the design of your flowers and hearts. When you are happy with the arrangement, cut two 6-inch squares of the clear adhesive paper. Take the backing off 1 piece, and lay it sticky side up on the table. Carefully arrange the hearts and flowers on the sticky side of the paper. Put a 12-inch piece of colorful satin or metallic cord on the bookmark so there is a small loop above the flowers and some of the cord hangs down from the heart and flower arrangement. Weight the hanging end of the cord with a large paper clip. Take the second sheet of contact paper, remove the backing, and cover the other side of your design. Remove the paper clip.

Cut away the excess contact paper, leaving behind your design and the bookmark cord. Your mother will read the love that went into your gift.

DANDY DESK ORGANIZER

Dad will love this dandy desk organizer for Father's Day—and you'll love making it!

WHAT YOU'LL NEED

Cereal box
Construction paper
Transparent and
    colored tape or
    glue
Assorted cardboard
    food containers
    (orange juice
    cans, small
    cereal boxes,
    etc.)
Scissors
Stickers
Markers or crayons
Other craft supplies

Use tape or glue to cover a large cereal box with colored paper. Arrange the assorted food containers on the cereal box, and carefully trace the outlines. Cut out each shape so the containers will fit into the cereal box.

Cover the containers with colored paper, insert them in the cereal box, and glue or tape them in place. Now decorate everything; you can use stickers, markers, crayons, construction paper cutouts—anything you think Dad would like!

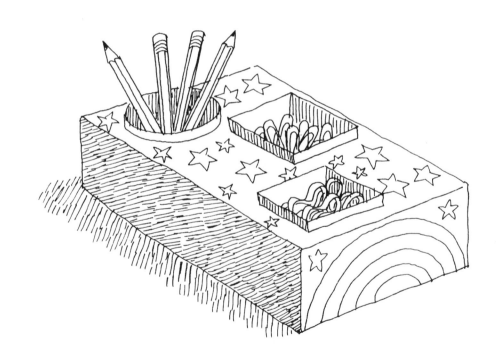

"A HUG FOR YOU" CARD

*Give your dad a double hug—one for real and
one he can carry around with him all day.*

**WHAT YOU'LL
NEED**
Construction paper
Scissors
Markers
Craft glue

Give Dad a card that is also a hug!

To make the card, cut out a large plate-sized head shape and draw on hair and a face so that it looks like you. Cut out an 18×4-inch rectangle. This will be the arms. Glue the head to the middle of the arms.

Now trace around your hands on a separate sheet of paper, and cut out the hand shapes. Glue a hand to the end of each arm. Fold the arms in so that the hands overlap. Inside the arms write a message for Dad, such as "Here is a big loving hug for you on Father's Day!"

The only thing he could like better than this card is a real hug to go along with it!

HERE IS A BIG LOVING HUG FOR YOU ON FATHER'S DAY

DAD'S BOOKMARK

For Father's Day, make Dad his own special bookmark.
He'll love it!

WHAT YOU'LL NEED

Self-hardening clay
Large paper clip
Craft glue
Paint
Paintbrush

Does Dad have a favorite hobby or activity? Is he a golfer, fisher, gardener, or bowler? Well, make a craft that is suited to your dad's special interests. He'll know you really care because you went to so much trouble to really think about what he likes.

Using the self-hardening clay, make the object that you want to be on top of the bookmark—maybe a bowling ball, a fish, a golf ball, or anything you think Dad would like! Push the nonclipping end of the paper clip into the back of the clay object. Let the clay dry.

Once the clay is dry, add some craft glue where the clay meets the paper clip to hold the clay in place. When the glue is dry, paint the clay any way you'd like. Is Dad's favorite color red? Paint a red fish—remember, you can use your imagination to create this bookmark. Realism is great, but fanciful is also wonderful!

For more colorful bookmarks, use colored paper clips that match or coordinate with the colors you want to paint the clay. These bookmarks would also make great birthday, thank you, and holiday gifts for every member of your family and all your friends!

GINGERBREAD AIR FRESHENER

*This air freshener makes the perfect gift for Father's Day!
Dad's car or truck will smell great with this hanging
from the rearview mirror.*

WHAT YOU'LL NEED

Sandpaper
Cookie cutter
Pencil
Scissors
Cinnamon sticks
Cheese grater
Clear glue (optional)
Twine or ribbon

On the smooth side of a piece of sandpaper, place a gingerbread man cookie cutter. Trace the shape with a pencil, and cut out the gingerbread man from the sandpaper.

Over the rough side of the sandpaper, grate a cinnamon stick with a cheese grater. (Be careful when you grate; you don't want to scrape your knuckles on the grater.) The cinnamon should stick in the crevices of the sandpaper, but you can also spread a little clear glue on the sandpaper before you grate the cinnamon.

Use the scissors to punch a small hole in the top of the gingerbread man's head. Put a piece of twine or ribbon through the hole so you can hang Dad's new air freshener on the rearview mirror of his car or truck.

HIGH-FLYING ROCKET

Launch a patriotic rocket in your own backyard!

WHAT YOU'LL NEED

Plastic drinking
straws
Scissors
Long red, white, and
blue balloons
Rubber bands
Paper
Ruler
Markers
Pencil

This balloon rocket will fly high in the air, just like fireworks.

To make a rocket, cut a straw in half. Fold the tip of 1 straw in half, and insert it into the end of the other straw half until it is all the way inside. Slide the neck of a balloon over 1 end of your double straw, and secure it with a rubber band.

Cut a 3-inch square piece of paper, and fold it in half. This will be your rocket's fin, which you can decorate with patriotic designs. Use a pencil to poke a hole through the middle of the fin, and slide it over the double straw.

To make your rocket fly, hold the rubber band around the balloon's neck and blow through the straw. When the balloon is full of air, let your rocket go! Make sure that no one is in the way before you let go. Your rocket should fly high. Experiment with different shapes and sizes of rocket fins. The fin controls the rocket's path.

Get your friends together for some high-flying fun! (Balloons are choking hazards—be sure to keep them away from small children! Discard all broken balloons immediately.)

GLITTERWORKS

Capture the feel of the rocket's red glare
without ever lighting a match.

WHAT YOU'LL NEED

Newspaper
Black construction
   paper
Pencil
Glue
Glitter
Fireworks designs

Many people love fireworks. They are part of what makes July 4 so exciting. So why not express your love of those explosive sky lights with glitter?

Cover your work surface with newspaper. Be creative—try to draw your favorite fireworks display using black construction paper and a pencil. The pencil marks will show a little—as shiny imprints. Trace your explosion with a thin line of glue. Sprinkle glitter on the glue. Let the glue dry for 5 minutes, then carefully shake the excess glitter off the page and into the glitter container to recycle it.

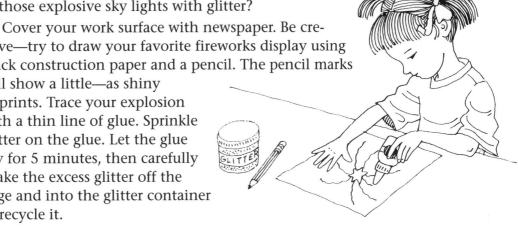

SPOOKY PICTURES

These are the scariest pictures you'll ever make by
blowing through a straw!

WHAT YOU'LL NEED

Newspaper
Drawing paper
Teaspoon
Thinned tempera
   paint
Drinking straw

These spooky pictures can be a little messy to make, so cover your table with newspaper before you begin. For each picture, pour a teaspoon of tempera paint onto a piece of paper. Gently blow at the paint through a drinking straw to make weird, scary shapes. If you want, you can add teaspoons of different colors of paint on top of the first color. These pictures will always be a big surprise. Is that a spider? Is that a witch riding a broom? Take turns with your friends describing the things you see in each picture.

CANDY SKELETON

This minty ghoul will be a favorite . . . until you gobble him up.

This cute little bag of bones is not only fun, he's almost edible—but you might not want to eat him after handling his "bones." So dig in for some graveyard delights.

Bend a chenille stem in half. Cut a skull out of white paper, and use a black marker to give him features. Slip 3 candies down the chenille stem to the center of the skeleton's body. These will be his ribs. Below the candies, pull the legs out so the candies stay on the body.

Wrap a second chenille stem just above the candies to form bony arms. Put a white gumdrop on the end of each leg for feet. Glue the paper skull to the top of the chenille stem (where it is bent in half), and the magic is complete.

This ghoul is sure to make your holiday decorations more festive!

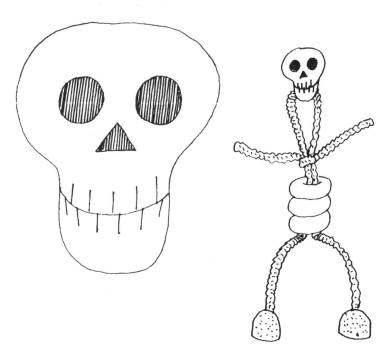

PITCH THE PUMPKIN GAME

*If you've ever wanted to catch the Halloween spirit,
here's your chance.*

MEDIUM

Adult Help Needed

WHAT YOU'LL
👀 NEED 👀
2 bleach bottles
Heavy-duty scissors
Permanent markers
Self-sealing sand-
    wich bags
Dry beans
Measuring cup
Fabric
Rubber band

Wash the bleach bottles well, and dry them. Have an adult help you cut the handles from the bottles to form catcher's scoops. Decorate the handles with permanent markers.

Fill a sandwich bag with 1 cup of dry beans, and seal the bag. Using scraps of Halloween fabric, wrap the bag in the fabric and use a rubber band to hold the fabric in place. (If you don't have Halloween fabric, use markers to decorate plain white fabric in a fun Halloween style.)

You're ready to start your game. Toss and catch the beanbag with your scoops. Whoever drops the beanbag first loses a piece of Halloween candy.

MUMMY PIN

Wear this silly, scary pin when you go trick or treating.

EASY

WHAT YOU'LL NEED
Wooden craft stick
White embroidery floss
Craft glue
2 wiggle eyes
Jewelry pin

You can make this pin almost as quickly as you can say the word "Mummy."

Wind white embroidery floss around a craft stick over and over. The more floss you wind on, the fatter your mummy will be! Make sure you wrap more floss around the middle. When you are finished winding, use glue to fasten the floss end to the back of the mummy. Glue 2 wiggle eyes to the front of the mummy, and glue a jewelry pin on the back.

Make a whole group of mummy pins, and pin them in a big "M" shape on the back of your Halloween costume. M is for Mummy!

TINY TURKEY PILLOWS

Place these tiny pillows on the couch or an easy chair for a soft, turkey touch.

MEDIUM

WHAT YOU'LL NEED

Old knit glove
Cotton balls or batting
Glue
Clothespins
Craft feathers
Yellow and red felt
Scissors
2 wiggle eyes
Fabric paint

These soft little pillows are just the thing to brighten up the furniture during the Thanksgiving season.

To make your turkey pillow, stuff an old knit glove with cotton balls or batting until it is full. Glue the bottom edges together. Hold the edges shut with clothespins until the glue dries.

Glue colorful craft feathers between and around the fingers of the glove. Cut a beak from yellow felt and a wattle (the turkey's red throat) from red felt. Glue them on the side of the thumb. Decorate your bird by gluing on wiggle eyes. You can also paint details on the turkey's body with fabric paint.

You might want to paint a name on your turkey. How about Tillie? Terwilliger? Thomasina?

TABLETOP GOBBLER

Make an edible centerpiece for your Thanksgiving table!

EASY

Adult Help Needed

WHAT YOU'LL NEED
Apple
Orange slices,
    raisins, cranber-
    ries, carrots,
    celery, and other
    fruit you'd like
    to use
Knife
Toothpicks

Place the apple on a table with the stem on the table. This is the body of the turkey. Have an adult help you cut up the fruit and vegetables you have chosen. Then start working on your turkey. Use the toothpicks to stick the pieces onto the turkey.

He needs a tail, a head, a wattle (the red thing that hangs down his neck), a beak, eyes, feet, and anything else you can think of. Use your imagination, and don't worry if your turkey doesn't look like the real thing. It will be a wonderful decoration for your table! And you can eat your turkey for a healthy snack. (Note: Don't eat the cranberries; they are very tart.)

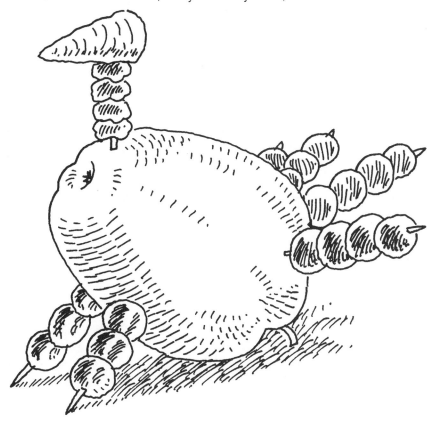

THANKSGIVING NAPKIN RINGS

These napkin rings are a perfect addition to the
Thanksgiving table.

WHAT YOU'LL NEED

Paper towel tubes
Ruler
Scissors
Construction paper
Craft glue
Craft supplies
   (markers, paint,
   paintbrush,
   ribbon, beads,
   feathers, etc.)

Measure and cut the tubes so each ring measures 2 inches in length. (Make enough so everyone coming to dinner has a napkin ring.) Cut the same number of 2-inch-wide colored paper strips. Glue the paper strips to the tubes.

Now decide how you want to decorate your napkin rings. You could make each different, or you could make them all the same. Draw a turkey, autumn leaves, pumpkins, or something else you're thankful for on construction paper, and cut it out. Glue it to the ring. Use markers, paint, ribbon, beads, and feathers to decorate the rings. Here is your chance to be really creative and fanciful.

How about drawing pictures of each family member for their own personalized napkin ring! Your artwork will be the talk of the table.

A Regular Holiday

Today, Thanksgiving is celebrated every year on the fourth Thursday of November. But did you know that the holiday was not celebrated every year after the first Thanksgiving, in 1621? Two hundred years after that first Thanksgiving, in 1863, Abraham Lincoln made it a national holiday.

INDEX

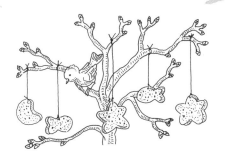

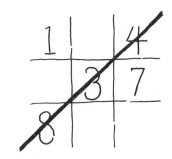

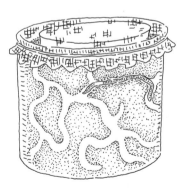

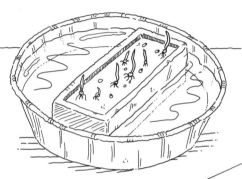